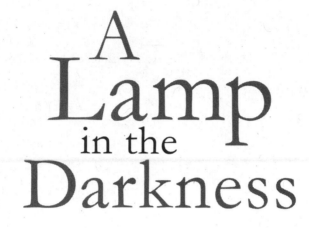

A
Lamp
in the
Darkness

Also by Jack Kornfield

A Lamp in the Darkness

Illuminating the Path Through Difficult Times

Jack Kornfield

SOUNDS TRUE
Boulder, Colorado

Sounds True, Inc.
Boulder, CO 80306

Published 2011

Page 24: From "Readers Write: Fears and Phobias" by D. S. Barnett in *The Sun* magazine (February 2002,
issue 314). Copyright © by D. S. Barnett. Reprinted by permission of the author.

Pages 70–73: Excerpt from *Mortal Lessons: Notes on the Art of Surgery* by Richard Selzer. © 1974, 1975, 1976,
1987 by Richard Selzer. Reprinted by permission of Georges Borchardt, Inc., on behalf of the author.

Guided versions of the meditations "Zen of an Aching Heart" and "Your Highest Intention" are
available at SoundsTrue.com/bonus/Jack_Kornfield_dark

Cover and book design by Jennifer Miles
Printed in Canada

Library of Congress Cataloging-in-Publication Data

Kornfield, Jack, 1945-
A lamp in the darkness : illuminating the path through difficult
times / by Jack Kornfield.
    p. cm.
ISBN 978-1-60407-448-2 (alk. paper)
1. Religious life--Buddhism. I. Title.
    BQ5410.K67 2011
    294.3'4442--dc22
                            2011010339
eBook ISBN 978-1-60407-642-4

10 9 8 7 6 5 4 3 2 1

To the
unquenchable human spirit
born anew
in each child.

This spirit
which has carried
Nelson Mandela,
Aung San Suu Kyi,
and so many others
through great hardship
will carry you.

Trouble? To live is to have trouble.
—Zorba the Greek

CONTENTS

Foreword

Entry points onto the path of Dharma are ubiquitously available yet mysteriously unpredictable as to when and where they appear to us. I imagine that just about every person who has ever been touched by the practice of mindfulness remembers with clarity and gratitude that first moment of connection with these teachings—which is never simply an introduction to the healing and transformative possibilities of the Dharma, but also, in essence, proffers a gentle reintroduction to oneself and to the possibilities for a veritable flourishing of one's life and heart.

This book is such an entry point. It is a beckoning source of both light and warmth, as its title suggests, inviting us into the cultivation of mindfulness and heartfulness through practice. It is the gift of a master teacher who has been responsible in large measure, along with a relatively small group of colleagues, for the introduction of mindfulness meditation practice in all its forms into American and Western culture over the past forty years.

Jack Kornfield is one of the great mindfulness teachers of the present day. His skill in inspiring people to practice is unsurpassed, as is the precision of his meditation instructions and the breadth and depth of his understanding. Beyond all that, he is best known and loved for the qualities of his heart, for his gentleness and kindness, for his compassion and caring, and for his willingness to be vulnerable and quintessentially real. The vast scope of Jack's rich and varied embodiment of wisdom, which is tailored to our present day and circumstance, is artfully condensed in this volume, a new portal through which to enter the world of meditative awareness and what it has to offer, especially in times of great difficulty when the mind so easily falls into darkness and feelings of unworthiness.

And the beauty of it is that not only can we read Jack's words, but that he is present through his verbal guidance on the audio versions of the meditation instructions. His voice rounds out and amplifies the gift of non-separation, where one comes to see that the deepest and most fundamental connection is not with the teacher, however great and skillful he might be, but with oneself in one's own fullness, a fullness that is not often recognized at first. In the poet T. S. Eliot's words, it is a fullness that is "Not known, because not looked for"—but finally, hopefully, "heard, half-heard, in the stillness / Between two waves of the sea." That stillness, that recognition, that clarity, that potential for reconnecting in the deepest of ways with one's own beauty, one's own genius, however much unrecognized or denied, is what is offered here in these highly nuanced practices aimed at giving yourself back to yourself, which is what so many people say is what they receive from their mindfulness practice.

With that in mind, may this entry point be one of miracle and wonder for you. May your experience of the practice lead to a re-befriending of yourself and a reigniting of passion for the life that is yours to live and for the path that is yours to walk—day and night, through thick and thin—in all the seasons of a life.

Jon Kabat-Zinn, PhD,
author of *Wherever You Go, There You Are* and
Mindfulness for Beginners
June 2011

Introduction

An Invitation to Awaken

I saw a cartoon in the *San Francisco Chronicle* that showed a family crossing the Sahara desert on camels. The father was on the first camel with his rugs and bags, the mother on the second, and three children were on smaller camels behind them. The last little girl and the father were obviously having a dialogue and the father looked back and shouted to her, "Stop asking if we're almost there yet—we're nomads for crying out loud!"

Every life is filled with change and insecurity, and every life includes loss and suffering and difficulties that arise regularly. We are all nomads in this ever-changing world, and we need ways to ground ourselves and remain centered no matter what happens.

When we encounter difficult times in our lives, it is not just the outer changes, but often our own state of mind that causes us the most difficulty. Grief and anxiety, fear and loss, and other turbulent emotions that we carry with us—and the stories we tell ourselves about the pains and trials of our lives—can contribute to our suffering and illness—until we learn how to release them.

Often, our initial strategy is to simply run away. But we find that our troubles follow us. Paradoxically, one of the best ways to heal from emotional betrayal and abuse, from injury and illness and trauma, is to turn toward that which is injured within us. In fact, when we bring a caring and fearless attention to that which is injured and difficult, these very circumstances often offer us important lessons and even surprising gifts that will transform our lives.

1

Do not be afraid to face your difficulty. Turn toward it. Lean into the wind. Hold your ground.

It is important to remember that the healing journey is not always about overcoming the difficulties we're experiencing or about getting well, at least not completely. It sometimes requires learning to accept more fully the way things are, bringing a wise and compassionate spirit to the circumstances of our lives. We all have the capacity to heal, but we have to discover what form that healing is to take.

By working with the teachings and meditations included in this book and audio, you will begin to trust the life force within you and learn the skills you need to transform your difficulties into a lamp that will guide you—and others—through the rest of your life.

CHAPTER ONE

The Wisdom of Our Difficulties

*There is praise and blame, gain and loss, pleasure
and pain, fame and disrepute. Did you think this
would not happen to you?*

The Buddha

If you're reading these words, you've probably hit hard times. Perhaps
you've lost a loved one, or maybe you've lost your job, or received a
difficult diagnosis, or someone close to you has. Maybe you're divorc-
ing or you're in bankruptcy or you've been injured, or your life is falling
apart in any number of ways. Maybe daily life itself has become too much
for you . . . or not enough. But even in the best of times there's plenty to
worry about: seemingly endless wars and violence, racism, our accelerating
environmental destruction. In difficult times, personally or collectively, we
often begin to wonder not only how we can get through this difficult patch:
we begin to question existence itself.

YOU ARE NOT ALONE

One of the most difficult things about hard times is that we often feel that
we are going through them alone. But we are not alone. In fact, your life
itself is only possible because of the thousands of generations before you,
survivors who have carried the lamp of humanity through difficult times
from one generation to another. Even Jesus had hard times, and Buddha did
as well. At times they were hounded, threatened, physically attacked, and

despised. Yet their gifts outshone all their difficulties. And now, as you read these words, you can feel yourself as part of the stream of humanity walking together, finding ways to carry the lamp of wisdom and courage and compassion through difficult times.

It's not about you. It's about us. Life is difficult for everyone.

Several years ago I was giving a talk on compassion with Pema Chödrön in a large hall in San Francisco filled with at least three thousand participants. At one point a young woman stood up and spoke in the most raw and painful way about her partner's suicide several weeks before. She was experiencing a gamut of complex emotions, such as agonizing grief and confusion, guilt and anger, loss and fear. As I listened to her I could feel her loneliness, and so I asked the group when she finished, "How many of you in this room have experienced the suicide of someone in your family, or someone really close to you?" More than two hundred people stood up. I asked her to look around the room at the eyes of those who had gone through a similar tragedy and survived. As they gazed at one another, everyone in the room could feel the presence of true compassion, as if we were in a great temple. We all felt the suffering that is part of our humanity, and part of the mystery that we share. But it's not only in great difficulties like the suicide of a loved one that we touch this truth: in the midst of our daily confusions, self-doubts, conflicts, and fears, we need support, reminders to trust in ourselves. We can trust. We were designed to journey through the full measure of beauty and sorrows in life and survive.

YOUR DIFFICULTIES ARE YOUR PATH

Grief and loss and suffering, even depression and spiritual crisis—the dark nights of the soul—only worsen when we try to ignore or deny or avoid them. The healing journey begins when we face them and learn how to work with them.

When we stop fighting against our difficulties and find the strength to meet our demons and difficulties head on, we often find that we emerge stronger and more humble and grounded than we were before. To survive our difficulties is to become initiated into the fraternity of wisdom.

The warrior in your heart says stand your ground. Feel the survival of a thousand years of ancestors in your muscles and your blood. You have all the support you need in your bones.

The real tragedy is when we refuse to acknowledge and respect our own suffering, and instead spread it unconsciously to others. As the Nobel Laureate Elie Wiesel has written, "Suffering confers neither privileges nor rights; it all depends on how one uses it. If you use it to increase the anguish of others, you are degrading, even betraying it...And yet the day will come ... when we shall all understand that suffering can elevate man as well as diminish him."[1]

AWAKEN THE ONE WHO KNOWS

The practices included in *A Lamp in the Darkness* are not positive thinking, quick fixes, or simplistic self-help strategies to navigate temporary difficult times. The practices here are profound tools for doing the work of the soul. They awaken your inner knowing. If you pay careful attention in the midst of your crises, you will begin to sense a witnessing consciousness, a wise presence inside of you that could be called "the one who knows." This knowing presence is consciousness itself, present in every moment of your life, even when it feels far away from you. Even in the toughest times of illness and loss, in your deepest depressions and griefs, underneath even your most catastrophic challenges and fears, the one who knows in you remains calm and clear. It already accepts whatever is going on. It sees beyond the immediate situation to something much larger. It knows that whatever change has come—no matter how much of a surprise it is to you—was

*Loss and betrayal tear
open the heart.
Look through this
gate for the wisdom
that lies there.
What matters now?
What would the wise
ones do now?*

going to happen. It knows that whatever is, *is*—whether we accept it or not. The one who knows is even often able to see grim humor in the most difficult situations. And it knows long before we do that the end of our suffering begins when we turn to face our suffering and embrace its truth and healing wisdom.

But how we can find this "one who knows" in the midst of our most overwhelming difficulties? Go to the mirror. Look at your face. You will see someone who looks older than you looked several years ago, although inside you don't feel any older. This is because it is only your body that has aged. The timeless awareness through which you see your body is the one who knows. Your body is only a temporary vessel for this awareness. It is a physical container for the undying consciousness of the one who knows.

LIVE IN THE PRESENT

You can learn to trust the one who knows, to experience consciousness as the space of awareness that is unchanging, independent of circumstance. It is open and clear and wise. Resting in the one who knows you can step outside of time, outside of endless worries about the future and the reruns of the past. The one who knows abides in the present moment.

The present moment is all we have, and it becomes the doorway to true calm, your healing refuge. The only place you can love, or heal, or awaken is here and now, the eternal present. Create life a day at a time. You cannot know the future. It is a mystery. But you can plant beautiful seeds here and now and learn to tend them with the love and courage and survival instinct that is inborn in you. Somerset Maugham once said, "There are three rules for writing the novel. Unfortunately, no one knows what they are." He wrote marvelous novels, the only way we can, a page at a time.

Whether your suffering stems from cancer or divorce or loss or conflict, the one who knows understands that it is only in the present that you can heal. The one who knows has the courage to acknowledge the way things are, and to care and love and trust, no matter what. The one who knows sees the bigger picture behind every illness, loss, and death. Wisdom knows that although you may feel that your life or another's life is ending, new life is always growing in and around you. The universe continues to expand, the Earth continues to turn through the seasons, the soil continues to bring forth new growth. Even in the moment of your eventual death, mothers will be giving birth, bringing new hope, love, difficulty, and possibility into the world.

Becoming aware and mindful, resting in the one who knows in the midst of your struggles, is not some magical cure. Your problems will not automatically and easily disappear. Being anxious and sad, angry and fearful, hurt, lost, and even despairing in difficult times is part of the natural process of suffering. Even being overwhelmed by challenging emotions is a natural part of the journey. If you judge yourself against some impossible ideal of how you think you "should" be feeling and acting as you struggle, you'll only add to your suffering.

If you can sit quietly after difficult news; if in financial downturns you remain perfectly calm; if you can see your neighbors travel to fantastic places without a twinge of jealousy; if you can happily eat whatever is put on your plate; if you can fall asleep after a day of running around without a drink or a pill; if you can always find contentment just where you are: you are probably a dog.

Being alive is finding ourselves in the midst of a great and mysterious paradox. The one who knows realizes that there are ten thousand joys and sorrows in every life, and at one time or another we will be touched by all of them. We will all experience birth and death, success and loss, love

Right now, how can these difficult emotions and thoughts and sensations become your path to liberation?

and heartbreak, joy and despair. And in every moment of your life there are millions of humans just like you all over the world who are being confronted by situations that are equally overwhelming and are struggling to somehow learn how to survive them. As George Washington Carver said, "How far you go in life depends on your being tender with the young, compassionate with the aged, sympathetic with the striving, and tolerant of the weak and the strong . . . because some day in life you will have been all of these."

YOU WILL SURVIVE

One of the world's greatest examples of how to survive difficult times is Nelson Mandela, the first president of modern South Africa. After twenty-seven years of imprisonment on Robben Island, he remained unbowed and dignified, gracious, tender and kind, and curious about everything that was happening around him. The one who knows inside him never took what was happening to him personally. In this way he was able to maintain his freedom even while in bondage, to retain his dignity even in the most degrading conditions, to continue practicing compassion in the face of hostility, and to respond to the hatefulness that surrounded him with an unwavering love. Although a solitary man jailed in a distant country, Nelson Mandela has become an inspiration for millions of people suffering through less dramatic but equally challenging situations. The one who knows in Nelson Mandela is the same one who knows inside you. You were born with the same potential for wisdom, the same insight, the same strength and love, all that you need to carry you through the difficulties that you encounter.

To heal, you must remember who you really are. Then no matter what happens to you, you can rely on this innate courage, you can trust your own wise heart because nothing and no one can take them from you. You are free like Nelson Mandela.

One of my spiritual teachers, the Thai meditation master Ajahn Chah, used to ask me, "Which has had more value in your life, where have you grown more and learned more, where have you become more wise, where have you learned patience, understanding, equanimity, and forgiveness—in your hard times, or the good ones?" When we come to understand the paradox that what we most value in our lives was often born out of conflict and struggle, we can begin to get a glimmer that perhaps one day we may begin to embrace our difficulties and find grace in them, even if that day is not today.

As you become intimate with your suffering, your heart grows tender.

Even the worst losses become workable over time. They become part of your life story and destiny; they become an important part of who you have become. Through surviving our difficulties, tenderness and compassion naturally arise. Your hardships are not only something intensely personal and intimate but also something you share with the entire world. Everything you have survived is responsible for who you are today. It is part of your heritage and cannot be taken from you; it lives in you in the same mysterious way that everything and everyone you have ever lost remains alive and present in your heart.

It's important to remember that even with the best of healing practices, your personal healing may not be easy. Turning to face difficult times can bring us face to face with the larger pains and fears beneath our grieving, or open a well of loneliness we have been running from our whole lives. But the practices in this program are designed to work with it all, to return you to acceptance and forgiveness and compassion—especially for yourself, so that you can hold everything in *yourself* with great mercy through these difficult times.

OPEN TO VASTNESS

You may not see it now, but this very difficulty will strengthen you. Your heart will grow wiser, your spirit stronger. You already know this. You can even begin to see the ways that this is true.

These practices will reconnect you to a bigger perspective of space and timelessness, so you can see everything with the eyes of the one who knows life's vastness and mystery.

You've had many tastes of the ever-present mystery and beauty of existence: when you've fallen in love or been present at the birth of a child, or in the timeless silence when you first saw the Grand Canyon or looked through a telescope at the stars and galaxies. In those moments your concerns were not with your difficulties. You were a conscious part of the miraculous eternal present moment.

Eternity is here, always, waiting in the present moment. We must learn how to return to the reality of the present moment even in our most difficult times. In the present moment we can learn to see clearly and kindly. With the great power of this mindfulness, we can become fully present to the unbearable beauty and the inevitable tragedy that makes up every human life. And we can honorably and fully experience this one and only life that we have been given, with all its ups and downs. In my own life, I try to remember the words many of us have heard from the Ojibway Indians: "Sometimes I go about pitying myself when all the while I'm being carried by great winds across the sky."

TRUST

The practices offered here are given with an open hand. They can bring healing and transformation to both your body and your mind. They will give you the tools for trusting the natural unfolding of your life and reconnect you to the unstoppable power of renewal that is always waiting to break through, no matter what your current difficulties. Try each of them and trust yourself to know which ones suit your heart and your current predicament. Perhaps others will become more useful to you at other times.

Remember, too, that although these practices can bring genuine healing from your present difficulties, more difficulties will come. It is the nature of life for difficulties to arise, and there are new challenging times yet ahead. This is our human lot, and our calling. It is how we grow. As Michael Jordan said, "I've missed more than nine thousand shots in my basketball career, I've lost almost three hundred games, twenty-six times I've been trusted to take the game-winning shot and missed. I've failed over and over again in my life, but I still keep going out on the court. And that's why I succeed."

As you go through this difficult time, sense how many other people on this earth are facing the same problems: loss, conflict, divorce. Feel your common humanity with them. When you can awaken sympathy, courage often follows.

By learning the skills in this book, I hope that when future difficulties arise, your path of healing will not be as long or dark. For just as it is certain that each life will include suffering, it is also true that in every moment there is the possibility of transcending your difficulties to discover the heart's eternal freedom. Your unshakable spirit waits to rearise. For, as the poet Pablo Neruda has written, "You can pick all the flowers, but you can't stop the spring."

CHAPTER TWO

The Earth Is My Witness

Make your mind like the earth which receives all things steadily.

The Buddha

Years ago, a crew of Russian cosmonauts ran into trouble in their space station. After a long and frightening period of uncertainty, they eventually found a way to safely return to Earth. When their capsule finally landed, they got out and knelt down and kissed the ground.

The Earth that they kissed is every living thing's true home. It is from the elements of the Earth that we are given birth, and it is the fruits of the Earth that nurture us so that we can live and grow. The Earth is the foundation for our houses, for our communities, for our civilizations. It is on the surface of Earth that we walk, and it is on the solidity of the Earth that we lie down to sleep. And eventually, when we cease to live, we will return to the Earth, in one way or another.

On the night when Buddha vowed to remain in meditation until he became enlightened, it was on the Earth that he took his seat. And as he sat under the bodhi tree, all of his fears and doubts, all of his temptations and desires arose in him. The story tells that these difficulties arose in the form of Mara, an Indian demon who personifies doubt, difficulty, evil, terror, and temptation. And when the armies of Mara were at their strongest and the temptations were at their greatest, Mara challenged Buddha's worthiness, asking him, "Who do you think you are to sit on this spot and seek enlightenment?" Reconnecting with his dedication and compassion, Buddha reached down and put his hand

The path through trouble is always made a step at a time, a breath at a time, a day at a time.

upon the Earth and said, "The Earth is my witness." In his extremity, Buddha called upon Earth to be the true witness to his value as a human being and his right to awaken upon that seat, supported by the Earth itself.

When our inherent value and dignity as human beings is witnessed, whether by the Earth or by those around us, it can transform our life. A math teacher in Indiana once had a class filled with raucous and difficult students, as every teacher has had at some time in their career. On one of those particularly trying days right before vacation, she realized that no one was going to be learning much math, so she stopped the class and wrote on the board the names of the thirty-one students and asked everyone to copy them onto a sheet of paper. Then, after they had all copied them down, she gave them fifteen minutes to write next to each student's name something that they admired about that person. She then collected the pages and dismissed the class. Some months later when the class was again having a hard time paying attention, she stopped the class and said, "I have something to pass out to you." She had cut the pages apart and pasted under each student's name the admiring comments that their classmates had written.

Several years after that, she received a call from the mother of one of her favorite students. After graduating high school, he had enlisted in the army and was killed in the Middle East. His mother asked if his favorite teacher would come to the funeral. At the end of the ceremony when they stood around the gravesite to honor his life, his mother walked up to the teacher and said, "My son had very few things with him when they found his body, but this was in his pocket." She took out the piece of paper that had the list of thirty-one good things written about him by his classmates. It had obviously been folded and unfolded many times. Then the young woman standing next to the teacher, who had been a student in the same class, said;

"Oh, yes, I carry mine too. I look at it when things get hard," and pulled hers out of her wallet. And another young man nearby said, "I made mine part of my wedding vows."

Neither avoid nor overreact. Tend what you are given. Stay centered in yourself.

Being reminded of our dignity and value is the ground for wisdom and compassion to arise. With this presence we will have the courage to touch our pain, our losses, our fears, our wounds and illnesses. When we experience feelings of unworthiness, frustration, and sorrow, our difficulties, struggles, and challenges can be held with dignity and awareness.

In the practice of "The Earth Is My Witness," we will learn how to take a seat on the Earth and become the mindful witness of all that arises. Meditation teacher Tamara Engle, while sick with cancer, wrote about the dignity and trust she learned from this practice of mindful witnessing:

> My days are short and as I grow weaker, I experience so much gratitude for my meditation. Not only the joy and ease it brought, but the hard parts. For every bored and restless sitting and every fearful fantasy, and every pain and ache I sat through, and every itch I witnessed and did not scratch, was a training for kindness. A training for the muscles, for bearing witness, for the trusting spirit that carries me now, even as I face my death.[1]

We have the capacity to take our seat under our own tree of enlightenment in the midst of all things in this world and to be present for them with clear eyes and an open heart. In the midst of your difficulty, you will learn the true strength of meditation. Zen master Suzuki Roshi has written:

> Suppose your children are suffering from a hopeless disease, you do not know what to do, you cannot lie in bed. Normally the most comfortable place for you would be a warm comfortable bed, but now because of your mental agony, you cannot rest. You

Be the potter of your life. Center yourself on the wheel. Find the still point.

may walk up and down, in and out, but this does not help. Actually, the best way to relieve your suffering is to sit . . . even in such a confused state of mind and bad posture.[2]

To carry the lamp through the darkness you need firm footing—ways to become centered and stable and grounded in the midst of your most challenging difficulties. The practice of "The Earth Is My Witness" starts with taking your seat. Established in the here and now, you can begin to become the witness to things as they are.

As you take your seat in this meditation, your mind and body will experience the power of accepting things as they are, no matter how painful or challenging. In practicing in the midst of your difficulties, you will find your inner strength, the courage that has brought you this far. This is all you'll need to overcome your present difficulties as well.

Meditation Practice
The Earth Is My Witness

 This meditation is included as Track One on the audio portion of this program.

Sit in a way that is comfortable and stable, with a sense of ease and dignity. Be still and alert, mindful as you take your seat on the Earth.

After you've taken your seat and feel stable, take several deep breaths to release any obvious tension you're carrying, so that you can be even more fully present.

Like Buddha on the night of his enlightenment, consciously acknowledge your place on the Earth. Let the Earth become witness to your right to be here as a human being. Feel yourself grounded and stable in your posture. Feel the support of the Earth as you sit upon it, and at the same time feel yourself as a part of the Earth, solid like a mountain and rooted as if your roots go down into the Earth, all the way to the center of the Earth.

Now, in the first part of this practice, release your burdens as you sit firmly seated on the Earth, solid like a mountain. Begin to release the burdens and difficulties that you carry, and let them return to the Earth.

Bring your attention first to your head. Become aware of the great river of thoughts, plans, and memories, the expectations and fears. Let all these drain down through your body back into the Earth. Feel any tension in your face—the unwept tears behind your eyes, the tension of fear and anger in your jaw—and let this too drain down through your body back into the Earth.

Now roll your head in a circle and feel all the cares carried in your neck begin to flow down through your body and back into the Earth. Now release whatever weight you carry in your shoulders—the backpack of tensions, the heaviness, the tightness—let them flow down through your body and back into the Earth.

Now relax your arms and feel how they've carried your struggles, your needs, your conflicts, your difficulties. Release all of their tension down through your elbows, your wrists, your hands, your fingers, and as you touch the Earth, let the tensions you have held drain out of your body back into the Earth.

Now bring your attention to the front and back of your chest, and your great heart within. Feel the burdens, aches, betrayals, and longings you carry there, and one by one release these too into the Earth. Take your time. Let your heart soften and your chest open and feel your breath come freely to fill the open space.

Move down now to your stomach and sense all that you hold there—all of the tightness around your anxiety and worry—and let it all release and drain down through your body into the Earth.

Now bring your attention down through your spine to your pelvis and genital area. Feel how your pelvis supports your torso, just as the Earth holds you. Notice how your spine and genitals and pelvis also carry tensions, burdens, fears, traumas, and conflicts. Let them all go and gradually drain through you and into the Earth.

Now bring your attention to your thighs and legs and feet that have carried and moved you and have absorbed so many of your tensions and burdens and difficulties. Slowly let these tensions and burdens and difficulties too drain into the Earth.

When you have released whatever tension you can from the whole of your body, sweep your attention from top to bottom. Feel the new clarity and steadiness and strength. Your body becomes present, unified, solid like a mountain. Let it rest on the Earth as if a part of the Earth. Become aware of the deep calm and restfulness that grows in your body as it clears. Let your mind quiet, and your heart open into silence and stillness. With the Earth as your witness, you can now sit as centered as Buddha—halfway between heaven and Earth in human form.

In the next part of this meditation, you sit like a Buddha, becoming a compassionate witness to all things. Start by resting in the space of mindful awareness. With this steady witnessing, become aware of the changing sensations in your body. Relax with them. After a time, notice the waves of your feelings and thoughts and the coming and going of sounds in your environment. Let all these experiences rise and fall like waves of the ocean while you rest in awareness itself. To steady this witnessing, notice the natural wave of the breath underneath all the other waves. Notice how your breath breathes itself. Feel its natural rhythm, its coolness in your nostrils, its tingling in the back of your throat, the rise and fall of your chest and belly.

> *It's not what you planned, but this is your life. You're still here. Listen. Something new is coming.*

And as you feel your breath come and go, let all the other waves of experience—the sensations, feelings, and thoughts—rise and fall like waves of the ocean around the breath. Become the witness of the breath and all that rises and passes away around the breath. If a strong experience carries your awareness away from your breath, let go of the breath and witness this new wave with the same spacious attention that you've given to your breath. As if to bow to it, name it gently: sadness or excitement, longing, planning, remembering, fear, tingling or coolness in the body, or sounds in your environment. Whatever arises, receive it with mindful and kind attention. Name it gently and feel the wave move through your body and mind, and then watch it pass away. And when it passes away, return to the breath and rest again in the open space of awareness. Let the body be solid like a mountain and the mind open like the sky. Rest on the Earth like a Buddha, and become acquainted with your capacity to witness all that arises, to remain centered and stable and steady in the midst of it all.

Return to this practice as often as it serves you. Make the practice of "The Earth Is My Witness" a way to steady and nourish yourself, to quiet your mind, to open your heart, to become wise in the midst of all of the changes you experience in your life.

CHAPTER THREE

Shared Compassion

Hold yourself as a mother holds her beloved child.

The Buddha

One recent student of mindfulness was a young army lieutenant who had been remanded to an eight-week class of mindfulness training by his commanding officer because of his inability to control his temper. After about six weeks of learning the practice of mindfulness and bringing a kind and compassionate attention to his experience, he found himself in a hurry, shopping at a local supermarket on his way home one evening. The market was crowded and the checkout lines were long. He had a full cart and noticed that the woman in front of him had only one item in her basket. This lieutenant was the kind of person who wanted things to be done right. She was in the wrong line. She was supposed to be in the express line. Worse than that, she was carrying a baby in her arms, and when she got up to the checkout clerk she held the baby up and the clerk began to coo and talk to the woman about the baby. And then, the woman handed the baby across the counter so that the clerk could hold him! A long line of people was waiting. The annoyance the lieutenant had been feeling built to a point where he was about to lose control and say something in anger to the two women. But after six weeks of training in mindful awareness, a part of him became aware that he was triggered.

The lieutenant decided to use this as an opportunity to try some of the mindfulness and attention practices he'd been learning. Bringing his

It is never too late to begin again. You can always make a fresh start.

attention to his breath, he began to experience a sense of spaciousness and release from his feelings of being overcome by his strong emotions. He did not push the irritation away; rather, he became aware of his anger and by honoring and accepting it, he felt enough of a release from his strong feelings to notice the waves of pain and heat and energy and judgment that were filling his body.

And, after taking a few more deep breaths, he felt a kindness begin to flood him and surround his pain and suffering until they slowly diminished. As he became filled with compassion, he looked up and realized that even though the woman was chattering and holding up the line, the child was cute and the three of them seemed to be enjoying this pleasant social moment. So when he got up to the checkout counter he'd calmed down enough to say graciously, "That was kind of a cute kid, wasn't it?" And the checkout clerk looked up at him and said, "Oh, do you think so? He's my boy. You see, my husband was in the army and he was killed in the Middle East last year. Now I have to work and my mom stays home to take care of my baby. She tries to bring him in once a day so I can see him."

We are so quick to judge one another. And just as we are hard on others we are even harder on ourselves. With mindfulness, our natural compassion grows. We can see that we are all carrying our own burden of tears. You and everyone you meet are sharing in some measure of the pain present on the planet. You are called upon to witness this pain—in yourself and others—with compassion. But how can we do this when we live in a time where it seems we have lost contact with the power of mercy and compassion, when we have closed off to the suffering of ourselves and others?

We have to begin to sense the tears for ourselves before we can cry for others. These tears are actually a great gift. They are the same moisture that brings new life out of the dry earth every spring. For the Lakota Sioux, grief is considered a great gift because they believe the gods are closest to us when we are suffering. When a Lakota Sioux has suffered a great loss and is grieving, he or she is considered *wacan*, or "most holy." Their prayers are believed to be especially powerful, and others will often ask one who grieves to pray on their behalf.

This doesn't mean that compassion will be easy, especially when you've been betrayed or you've suffered some irreplaceable loss. As the Sufis pray, "Overcome any bitterness that may have come because I am not up to the magnitude of the pain that has been entrusted to me."

You may want to heal, but still find yourself slipping

As you face loss, frustration, hurt, and conflict, invite a sense of your own dignity. Sit up, stand up tall. Have respect for yourself, and patience and compassion. With these, you can handle anything.

back into old habits of anger and resentment. This can be the most frustrating. After struggling for half a century with the British Empire, Mahatma Gandhi said that his most formidable opponent was not the British Empire or the Indian people, but a man named Mohandas K. Gandhi. "With him I seem to have very little influence."

But it is necessary to learn that you are worthy of being loved. Buddha put it quite simply: "You can search the whole tenfold universe and not find a single being more worthy of love and compassion than the one seated here—yourself." Self-compassion and self-forgiveness are not weaknesses, but the roots of our courage and magnanimity. Sometimes compassion for ourselves and others seems hard to find. But even if you lose touch with these feelings during your most intense suffering, compassion is an essential part of our true nature. In fact, it is in this self-compassion and self-love that you find the strength to carry the lamp through your darkest nights. And it is by first practicing self-compassion that you find not only a way to hold your own struggles and sorrows in your heart—but through them you learn how to connect with the sufferings and sorrows of all those around.

*You are more
than this hurt.
Remember who
you really are.*

This self-compassion helps us all survive. It causes us to jump out of the way of an unexpected fast car as we enter the street. We treasure our life. Self-compassion struggles to keep us alive even in situations of complete abandonment and abuse. D. S. Barnett wrote about such a situation in *The Sun* magazine:

My mother always assured me that unspeakable punishments were bound to befall any child as naughty as I was. "If I were you," she'd say, "I'd be afraid to go to sleep at night for fear God would strike me dead." She would speak these words softly, regretfully as though saddened by her errant daughter's fate. . . . [Mother went on,] "How could *anyone* ever love you?" It took me almost fifty years to heal the damage from all her ugly remarks. . . From the age of five or six, until I was well into my teens, whenever I had trouble sleeping, I would slip out from under my covers and steal into the kitchen for a bit of bread or cheese, which I would carry back to bed with me. There, I'd pretend my hands belonged to someone else, a comforting reassuring being without a name—an angel, perhaps. The right hand would feed me little bites of cheese or bread, as the left hand stroked my cheeks and hair. My eyes closed, I would whisper softly to myself, "There, there, go to sleep, you're safe now, everything will be all right, I love you."[1]

Even in a situation as desolate and difficult and inescapable as hers, compassion found a way to flow through her like an inner angel of mercy—like the green shoots that force their way through the cracks in the sidewalk.

As you go through your difficulties, you can learn to bring this same quality of loving care to everything you touch. In this practice, you will learn a systematic way to bring forth the quality of tenderness and compassion in any circumstance and situation. You will find that love and care have an extraordinary capacity to transform the sorrows of your life into a great stream of compassion.

Be gentle with yourself—it should not be a struggle. Know your limitations. Extend your compassion only as far as you feel your heart opening naturally. Plant your seed of trust. It will grow in its season.

Even in the ruins, some new life waits to be born. Fix the mast, or build a new ship.

Meditation Practice
Shared Compassion

This meditation is Track Two on the audio portion of this program.

Sit in a centered, grounded, and quiet way. Feel your body resting on the Earth—stable, present, gracious, and at ease. Feel your heartbeat, the flow of life blood within you, and how your breath moves softly in and out. Open to an appreciation for the fragility of life and how you naturally try to protect yourself in the face of your sorrows.

Begin the practice of generating compassion by starting with a person dear to you. Bring to mind someone close to you whom you love dearly. As you think of them, feel your love for them, the natural caring that arises within you. Take a few breaths. Now become aware of their struggles, sorrows, the losses and hurts that they experience in their life. As you become aware of their burdens and sorrows, notice how your heart naturally wants to extend comfort, to wish them well, to soothe their pain with your compassion.

To open further, begin to whisper in your own heart and mind some of the simple phrases of compassion. Picture this loved one and say softly, *"May you be held in* compassion. *May your pain and sorrow be eased. May you be at peace."* Allow your compassion to deepen as you spend some minutes continuing to repeat these phrases.

Now imagine that this same loved one has turned their caring gaze back to you. They are returning the feelings of care and love to you. Imagine them looking at you with compassion and love, aware of the measure of sorrows that you carry in your own life. Try to see yourself through their eyes. Imagine how they would feel if they were aware of all your suffering and struggles, your losses and betrayals, your fears and confusions, and your deep pain and injuries. Sense how their heart opens to you, their love transforming into natural mercy and compassion. Imagine they are returning your words, *"May you be held in compassion. May all your suffering and struggles be held in great compassion. May your pain and sorrow be eased."* Now recite these words for yourself: *"May I be held in compassion. May my pains and sorrows be eased. May I find peace."*

Breathe gently and stay with the practice of self-compassion for as long as you can. If it's helpful, you can place your hand on your heart as if you could touch yourself and all that you carry with the kindness of a Buddha. Spend ten minutes reciting these wishes for yourself. Feel the ease and the peace that comes as you offer these words of care over and over.

Let the spirit of self-compassion grow in you. Sense how you can carry the lamp of wisdom and compassion within your own heart. Know that you will get through your difficulties with dignity and your capacity to love. Know you will survive.

Then, when you feel ready, extend your compassion to others you know, one at a time. Let yourself envision loved ones, friends, and community members and hold the image of each of them in your heart. As you feel your love for them, become aware of their difficulties, their burdens, and their measure of sorrows. Wish them well. Repeat the same simple phrases of compassion for them: *"May you hold your sorrows and struggles in great compassion and kindness. May you be held in compassion. May your pain and sorrows be eased. May you find peace."* And, breathing gently, continue extending compassion to each loved one, or a whole group of loved ones and friends, holding them in tenderness.

When you're ready, open your compassion further to other groups of people. Gradually include friends and neighbors, then move on to extend compassion for your community, and then open your heart to the worldwide struggles of people, animals, to all beings who suffer in the world. Extend compassion to those who are easy to love, and then to those who are difficult, and finally even to those causing difficulties. Offer compassionate wishes for the brotherhood and sisterhood of all beings.

Feel the kindness in your heart grow. Envision that with each breath you can bring the sorrows and struggles of beings into your heart and, with each out-breath, extend yourself to wrap them in love and compassion with the words, *"May your sorrows be held in compassion. May your pain and struggles be eased. May your hearts be at peace."* Envision your heart as a purifying fire that can transform the suffering of the world into luminosity of compassion. Feel yourself to be a Buddha, a lamp radiating compassion to the world and its struggles.

And last, to complete the circle, bring compassion back to yourself. Hold yourself with the spirit of compassion, and silently repeat, *"Just as I wish well for all those around me, may I too be held in great compassion."* Feel this compassion for yourself in every cell of your body, in every part of your being. *"May my struggles and suffering be held in compassion. May my pain and sorrow be eased. May my heart be at peace."*

You can repeat and cultivate this practice of shared compassion as often as you'd like. If it feels difficult or you feel overwhelmed or lacking in compassion, don't judge yourself. Hold whatever is your experience in kindness. When you are ready, again continue to plant the seeds of compassion, for yourself and others. Remember that you are not trying to fix the pain of the world but only to meet it with a compassionate heart.

If you experience difficulties during this meditation, shift your attention to wherever compassion comes most naturally—to a child or a loved one or yourself. Work with simple phrases or change them to your own

It doesn't belong to only you. It's the dance of conditions. You can't choose the music, but you can choose how you will dance.

words and expressions of kindness. Gradually, you will learn to open your heart to everything that life brings. And whenever you encounter the sorrows of the world, and whenever you yourself enter hard times and difficulties, let this shared compassion be your response.

CHAPTER FOUR

Awakening the Buddha of Wisdom in Difficulties

Who is your enemy? Mind is your enemy.
Who is your friend? Mind is your friend.

The Buddha

I have on my refrigerator a picture of a solitary Chinese man returning from shopping with grocery bags in both hands, courageously blocking a row of military tanks in Tiananmen Square, unwilling to let them pass. We admire those who remain cool-headed in difficulties, those who carry the lamp of wisdom so beautifully in the world, and we are moved by images of dignity and courage like his. But that spirit is not only in him; it is in us too. Although we sometimes lose touch with it, we each have deep within us a lamp of wisdom, and a powerful spirit of compassion and conscience and understanding that we can draw upon.

To find this lamp, we must listen in a new way. Some years ago, one of the greatest primate biologists, George Schaller, came back from studying gorillas in Africa. Schaller was the mentor of Dian Fossey, who was portrayed by Sigourney Weaver in the movie *Gorillas in the Mist*. When Schaller returned from his field studies in Africa, he made a presentation at an important biological conference and talked about the familial patterns of the great apes. He spoke of the relationships between the young gorillas and their uncles and aunts, what the sibling relationships are, and

Pests, drought, animals, insects, no gardener gives up. Water, fertilize, plant new seeds. Whatever you plant and tend with care will bear fruit.

the role of the silverback male—all with rich detail and understanding that had never been known before. One of the professors at the conference asked, "Dr. Schaller, we biologists have been studying these creatures for several centuries and we did not know any of this. How did you get such detailed information?" And Professor Schaller answered, "It's simple. I didn't carry a gun."

Previous generations of biologists had gone into the mountains carrying large elephant guns because they were frightened of the huge and powerful gorillas. The gorillas sensed that these interlopers were scared and probably dangerous. But Schaller, wanting a genuine relationship to the gorillas, entered their jungle without any guns. Because he was unarmed, he moved slowly and deliberately, and the gorillas could sense the care and respect and openness and awareness in his relationship to them. And, after a time, because he posed no threat to them, they allowed him to sit in their midst and watch all of the activities of their family and tribe.

In the same way, the following practice will help you to learn how to bring this respectful attention and awareness to the most difficult situations in which you find yourself, and to your relationships with others. As you open to this illuminating consciousness beneath your struggles, a way through your difficulties will become clear.

This practice is quite simple, but because it involves visualization, some instructions about the visualization process itself are necessary. You won't be asked to visualize anything fancy in this exercise. A visualization practice simply asks you "to see with your mind's eye." You use this skill every day. When someone asks you to describe what you did on your last birthday, you will probably remember quite a bit without having to work very hard; the images will come naturally and easily to your mind's eye. You will see what you had to eat, where you were, who was with you, what gifts you received.

Visualization practice is the same. All you need to do is become aware of whatever comes easily and naturally to your mind's eye. The images may come to you as pictures, or they may be more of an intuitive knowing, or you may become aware of them as sensations in your body, or perhaps as feelings centered in the area of your heart. If you remain open to the experience, you will find your own way to use these practices to connect to the lamp of wisdom you carry deep within.

Meditation Practice
Buddha in Difficulties

 This meditation is Track Three on the audio portion of this program.

Sit in a way that is comfortable. Relax, be present, at ease, and alert. Feel your body resting on the Earth. Allow your breath to settle and rest in the present moment.

As you remain sitting, choose a circumstance in your life that is particularly difficult. Picture it clearly. Remember what it was like when you were back in the midst of this difficulty. Then imagine yourself back there. See with your mind's eye as many details as you can in your surroundings. Where are you? Are you with other people? Are you standing, sitting, lying down? Speaking, listening? Try to recall as many details as you can.

Now, become aware of the feelings that arise in you as you remember this scene. What does your body feel like? Notice the emotions and states of mind that you're experiencing at this time. Notice your level of tension or discomfort and how you respond to these feelings.

Continue to picture yourself in the midst of this difficulty. Notice what everyone else is doing or saying. Because this is only a visualization, you are completely safe, so although you may have experienced panic or discomfort, you are safe to imagine being in the situation. Be aware of your body, of your states of mind, and everything that is going on around you.

Now in the midst of this difficulty, if you are inside a house or office, imagine that there is a knock on the door. If you are outside, notice that someone at a distance is walking toward you. If you're with others, say, "Excuse me for a moment."

At first you won't know who is coming. Let it be a surprise. Pause, and then after a few moments when you open the door or the person comes closer to you, you will see that whoever has come is a marvelous wisdom figure, a luminous being who represents compassion and understanding and courage in difficulties. It might be Buddha or Kwan Yin, or it might be Mother Mary or Jesus or Solomon or Gandhi—a person or being who most represents compassion and wisdom to you. See who appears.

Imagine that this luminous figure can walk up to you and greet you and ask, "Are you having a hard day?" Feel the warmth and care in their smile. And then they say to you, "Let me help you. Let me show you how I would handle this. Give your body to me and I will enter it and look like you, and you can become invisible and follow along with me. No one will notice that I've entered your body."

Follow along with them back into the difficulty. Notice when they enter the situation how their body feels and what their states of mind and heart are in this difficulty. Notice how they listen and respond to the events and situations as they develop. Take your time. Let yourself visualize in any way you can what this luminous being in your body does. Notice how they act, how they bring wisdom and compassion to your difficult circumstances. Let them show you. Wait until they have completed all they can do for you in this particular situation. Then let them excuse themselves from the situation and follow them as they return back to where you met them.

Now they give you your body back and resume their original luminous form. Before they go, they want to offer you a gift. Visualize as they reach under their clothing and place this gift in your hand. It will be a clear symbol of exactly what you need to help in this difficulty. And if the symbol is not exactly obvious to you at first, hold it up to the light so you can see it better. Once you know what the gift is, thank them for it. Finally, before they go, they will touch you gently and whisper in your ear a few last words of advice. Let yourself hear or imagine or think of the words of advice from your wisdom figure. They will help you through your difficulties. After you receive this advice and the gift they have given to you, thank them sincerely for their help and let them go.

The past is gone. The future is not yet here. You can be present for this moment. What you do now will create your future.

Now return to the present moment and spend a moment reflecting on how they approached your difficulty and what they have taught you. Write down the words of wisdom and what you understand about the gifts they have given to you.

It is remarkable how quickly a wisdom figure will appear to most people. In a moment, a luminous being like Mahatma Gandhi or Mother Theresa or the Dalai Lama or an image of Jesus or Buddha or Kwan Yin will appear. Where do these wise beings and their gifts and words come from? Us! These are images of the innate understanding and compassion that we naturally carry within us. They are our own Buddha nature.

Having completed this visualization, reflect back. How did your body feel when you first entered your great difficulty? Did you feel tension, rigidity, fear, confusion, pain? Now recall how this wisdom figure's body felt as they entered the difficulty. The wisdom figures bring with them a sense of physical relaxation, centeredness, a graciousness. It is as if we already know what it feels like to bring graciousness, courage, and wisdom to our most difficult struggles.

Imagine you are Buddha in disguise. No one knows but you, but you know you must bring care and understanding no matter what. How can you accomplish this?

Remember too how carefully this luminous being listened in the midst of this difficulty, how they responded and acted. Feel how their love and strength came together. Their behavior will become a model for you the next time you find yourself in difficulty.

Reflect on the symbolic gift they gave you. It comes to you from the deepest levels of your psyche. Though often simple, people report that the gifts are the perfect symbol of what they need. Sometimes your receive a mirror, a sword, a crystal, a heart, or a feather. Whatever gift you receive, live with it for as long as you can until it gradually shows you its many meanings. Like an image from a dream, it is a symbol whose meaning may at first seem obvious, but whose deeper dimensions and importance will become clearer to you over time.

The understanding you experienced during this practice is already inside you. The insightful words come from your own spirit. Be sure to write the words down. Read them aloud to yourself, feel their resonance in your heart, and know that they are a message from your wisest self, the one who knows. Repeat them in the future as you face your most difficult times, for this is the message that will help carry you through even the hardest times.

Feel free to use this meditation as many times as you like. It is a practice that you can return to many times in many different ways. You can return to the same issue, or you can try it with other difficulties that you encounter or have experienced in the past. Other luminous figures may appear and additional gifts and information will come to you. Even if you are one of those who cannot visualize easily, allow this practice to work on other levels. Value everything you experience through any avenue of perception, for they all illuminate your inner wisdom. Respect whatever intuitions, subtle awarenesses, or knowings in your body you experience.

CHAPTER FIVE

The Practice of Forgiveness

He beat me, he robbed me, he hurt me.
Abandon these thoughts. Live in love.

The Buddha

As human beings, we are guaranteed at one time or another to suffer from betrayal, conflict, loss, and pain. We will encounter betrayal and conflict in our families and communities. At times, these difficulties can feel insurmountable and we long for a way out of the suffering and conflict. The first step we need to take is to protect ourselves and others, to set limits, to minimize harm. Then, what is also necessary for us to move forward through our pain is forgiveness—of ourselves and others, and of the events that have caused our suffering.

It's important to remember that forgiveness doesn't happen all at once. You can't achieve forgiveness by covering up your genuine hurt feelings. There are times when it is important to fully experience feelings of grief and rage and despair and pain before we can move on. Sometimes, there are also events in your life that you believe to be absolutely unforgivable. But sooner or later, for your own good, your heart will realize that you need to let go. As my friend and teacher Maha Ghosananda, the Gandhi of Cambodia, said to thousands of refugees who had suffered enormously, "Remember these teachings from Buddha, 'Hatred never ceases by hatred, but by love alone is healed. This is the ancient and eternal law.'"

Sometimes the only thing you can do is let it go. Start anew.

This instruction appeals to the nobility of our hearts. To find peace we must bring an end to hatred through love. "Oh nobly born," say the Buddhist texts, "remember who you really are. Know that a great and forgiving heart lies within you too." There is an awareness inside us—even in those who experienced the horrors of the Khmer Rouge and the killing fields in Cambodia—that as long as we harbor anger and resentment in our hearts we will never find peace. Without forgiveness, we are trapped in the past, carrying forward and repeating the sufferings we've experienced, from generation to generation. Without forgiveness, the Northern Irish Protestants and Catholics have continued their battles for centuries. Without forgiveness, the Hutus and Tutsis in Rwanda, the Bosnians and Serbs and Croats, the Palestinians and Israelis will continue to sentence their children and their children's children to generations of suffering and conflict. To free ourselves, each of us will have to say, "These cycles of suffering and retribution stop here, with me. I refuse to pass this suffering on to my children. I refuse to carry hate."

In this way, forgiveness is not primarily for others, but for ourselves. It is a release of our burdens, a relief to our hearts. A story I like to tell is about two ex-prisoners of war who met again years later. One said to the other, "Have you forgiven our captors yet?" And the second one answered through gritted teeth, "No, never." With this the first one looked at him kindly and said, "Well then, they still have you in prison, don't they?" Only by learning to forgive, can we let go of what is holding us back and move on with our lives. Forgiveness means giving up all hope for a better past.

Forgiveness is not a single act but a practice that one undertakes, sometimes over a long period of time. When one of my teachers taught me this forgiveness practice, he said, "Why don't you try it twice a day for five minutes, then after six months, let me know how it's going." I found that my understanding of this practice changed and deepened month by month. By the time the six months were completed, I realized that my teacher had asked me to practice forgiveness three hundred times before I evaluated its effects.

Release the past. Forgive yourself. Forgive others. Don't harden your heart.

What I discovered by practicing forgiveness over this period of time was that sometimes I felt true forgiveness in my heart, and sometimes I felt its opposite: deep resentment that I refused to let go. Sometimes I experienced pain and at other times I was overcome with rage and anger. But eventually tears would come that brought emotional healing. And little by little, the way water wears away a stone, the pain in my heart melted.

It is important to understand that forgiveness does not mean that you condone what happened. In fact, it often means that you have to do what is necessary to make sure it never happens again—to yourself or anyone else. But in the end, forgiveness also means not putting anyone out of your heart. Those who practice forgiveness know it is an act of courage. As the *Bhagavad Gita* says, "If you want to see the brave, look to those who can forgive."

I remember some years ago riding on the train from Washington DC to Philadelphia to attend my father's memorial service. I sat down next to an elegantly dressed man who told me in our conversation that he had quit his job for the State Department to work with youth in the inner city. His main project was to work with young men who were accused of murder. Then, he told me a story.

One young boy, just fourteen years old, wanted to become part of an inner city gang. In order to initiate himself into the gang, he went out and shot another teenager his own age. He was subsequently caught and arrested for the murder and, after a time, was brought to trial. He was convicted and just before he was taken off to prison, the mother of the young

Avoid harm, act with integrity. The best of your humanity can make itself known in your difficulties.

man who'd been murdered stood up in the courtroom, looked him square in the eye, and said, "I'm gonna kill you." And then he was led off in handcuffs.

While he was incarcerated, the mother of the young man who had been killed came to visit him. He was shocked and surprised. During her first visit she talked to him for a little while, and later she came back and brought him some things he needed—a little money to buy things in prison, some writing materials—and began to visit him regularly. And over the next three or four years, as he served his sentence, she would come visit him regularly.

When the time came for him to be released, she asked him what he planned on doing when he got out of jail. He had no idea. "Where are you going to work?" she asked him. He didn't know. So she told him, "I've got a friend who has a little business—maybe you could get a job there." And then she asked, "Where are you gonna live?" And he said, "I don't know. I didn't have much of a family even before I came in here." And she said, "Well, you can come and stay with me. I've got a spare room." And so the young man moved into her home and began to work at the job that she had found for him.

After about six months, she called him into the living room, sat him down, and said, "I need to talk to you." He said, "Yes, ma'am." She looked at him and said, "Remember that day in court when you were convicted of murdering my only child?" He said, "Yes, ma'am." She said, "Remember I stood up and I said, 'I'm going to kill you'?" He said, "Yes, ma'am." "Well, I have. I set about changing you. I came to visit you over and over and brought you things, and made friends with you. And when you got out, I took care of you and got you a job and a place to live, because I didn't want the kind of boy who could coldly murder my son to still be alive on this Earth. And I've done it. You're not that boy anymore. But now I have no son and I've got no one and here

38

you are and I wonder if you'd stay with me and live with me for a time. I can finish raising you as my son and I'd like to adopt you, if you'd let me." And she became the mother of her son's killer, the mother he never had.

For most of us, forgiveness will not be so dramatic, but in small ways and large, we all need to find the healing waters of forgiveness. We must start where we are: our own body and spirit and heart. However we can, we need to forgive, to wash away the anger and guilt and blame that we carry. And once we've learned how to forgive ourselves, we will be able to ask forgiveness from others for the ways we've harmed them out of our ignorance and suffering. And then we will be able to look with the genuine eyes of mercy upon those who have hurt us out of their own pain and ignorance, their anger and confusion. In that moment we will understand the true gifts and purpose of forgiveness—that it is never too late to forgive, that forgiveness is the only medicine that can release us from the past and allow us to truly begin anew.

Don't listen to those who stir you up. Don't listen to others who put you to sleep. Respect them all. Thank them all. Then remember, there is a bird singing only you can hear.

Meditation Practice
The Practice of Forgiveness

 This meditation is Track Four on the audio portion of this program.

Sit in a comfortable position. Allow your eyes to close gently. Rest for a moment and allow yourself to relax. When you are ready to begin, become aware of your breath and breathe for a few minutes as if you are breathing gently in and out of your heart. Now let yourself feel the emotions you still carry and the barriers you've erected within your heart because you have not forgiven. Some are the result of not forgiving others, and some are from not yet being able to forgive yourself. Let yourself feel the pain and constriction that comes from keeping your heart closed. As you breathe gently, follow the three steps of the practice of forgiveness.

First, ask forgiveness from others:

Reflect: *"There are many ways that I have hurt and harmed others, betrayed them, abandoned them, caused them suffering or pain, knowingly or unknowingly. I remember these injuries now."*

Let yourself visualize and remember the ways you've caused harm to others—one or two particular incidents or any number of them. Take as much time as you need to feel whatever memories burden your heart. Remember how your actions came from your own pain and confusion, your hurt and fear. Now allow yourself to feel the genuine sorrow and regret and pain you still carry. When you are ready, realize that you are finally able to release this burden and ask for forgiveness. After a few more breaths, silently repeat to yourself, *"In the ways that I have caused sorrow for you, knowingly or unknowingly, out of my own fear and confusion, out of my anger and hurt and suffering, I ask your forgiveness. Forgive me. Please forgive me."* As you ask for this forgiveness, gradually let yourself receive the blessing of forgiveness. Allow yourself to make amends, to let go, to move on with a heart freed from this burden. Sense that you can be forgiven.

The second direction of forgiveness is forgiveness for harming yourself:

Just as we have caused suffering to others, there are many ways that we have hurt and harmed ourselves. We hurt ourselves at the same time we hurt others. And in many other ways we abandon and betray ourselves. Take time to remember the ways that you've caused pain and suffering to yourself. You have harmed yourself, knowingly and unknowingly, in thought or word or deed. Feel the cost of this self-betrayal. Sense the ways you judge yourself about what you've done, recognize the pain, the sorrow, and the shame that you still carry in your body, heart, and mind. Realize that you are ready to release these burdens.

As you remember them, extend forgiveness for each act of harm in this simple way: *"For the ways I've hurt myself, betrayed or abandoned myself, caused myself pain as I have to others at times, through action or inaction, out of fear, confusion, hurt, anger, and ignorance, I now extend forgiveness to myself. I hold myself with mercy and tenderness. I forgive myself."* If it's helpful, you can place your hand on your heart to literally hold yourself with forgiveness at this point. Then continue to repeat, *"In the ways that I have caused pain and suffering out of my ignorance and fear, out of hurt and confusion, I offer myself forgiveness."* Let the healing balm of forgiveness touch every part and cell of your body. Let it wash over every story and feeling you hold in your heart. Ease your mind into the great heart of forgiveness. Breathe gently and continue this practice as long as you need to.

The third direction of forgiveness is forgiveness of those who have hurt or harmed you:

In this practice, it is very important not to be hurried, nor to expect that you can or should forgive others right away. For a time, the practice of forgiveness can bring up its opposite. You can experience layers of rage and grief and tears and sorrow and shame. Hold whatever happens during this part of the meditation with tenderness and forgiveness and mercy. And let this practice be a process of purification that will, little by little, cleanse your heart so that when you are ready, you will be able to release the past, and forgive even those who have harmed you, so that you can move on freely with your own life.

Begin this practice by repeating silently, *"There are many ways that I have been hurt or harmed by others, abused, abandoned, and betrayed—knowingly and unknowingly. I remember these occasions now."* Visualize the times in the past that you have been hurt by others, and feel the pain and sorrow you still carry. Then sense the burden of this pain you carry and resolve to release it by gradually extending your forgiveness to others as your heart is ready. When you are ready, repeat silently, *"I remember the many ways in which you have hurt or wounded or harmed me, abandoned or betrayed me. I know that you acted this way out of your own fear and pain, out of your hurt and anger and confusion. I've carried this pain in my heart long enough. To the extent that I am ready, I offer forgiveness to you who have caused me harm. I release you, I forgive you. As best as I can, I will not put*

Whatever is happening, tend your body and heart. When you feel overwhelmed move around, stretch, shake your body. Take three full breaths. Return to the present moment.

anyone out of my heart. I will release the past and start anew. While I cannot condone what you did and will do everything in my power to make sure no one is harmed by you again, now in this moment, I release you. I offer you forgiveness, so that I can move on."

Breathing gently into the area of the heart, continue with this third practice of forgiveness as long as it is helpful to you. Again and again, in a gentle and courageous way, liberate your heart, as you liberate others.

CHAPTER SIX

The Temple of Healing

Aging, sickness, and death are suffering.
To lose what you love is suffering.

The Buddha

We all need healing at different times in our lives. Sometimes we need healing for physical illness. At other times, we need to heal the traumas that we've suffered and find ways to release the difficulties of the past that we carry in our bodies. We need release from the struggles and emotions brought about by our conflicts and the pain we experience from the follies of humanity.

To heal we cannot reject our illness and grief or use anger and aversion to try to get rid of them. Instead, we have to bring a tender, healing energy to all that is sick or torn, what is broken or lost. In the Buddhist prayer of healing, similar to the spirit of Jesus, we recite: "May I be the healing medicine for all who are sick. May I bring healing to myself and others." We believe that healing is possible and dedicate ourselves to be part of that healing. We become tender and wise with ourselves and those around us, especially when we are experiencing fear and grief ourselves.

Sometimes this is all that healing asks, that we become present. A meditation practitioner once came to one of our two-month retreats at Spirit Rock after his four-year-old son had died in a car accident. This man, the father, had been driving. Immediately following the accident, he sought help by talking to a succesion of healers, shamans, and lamas, and being consoled by friends

Can you see how much suffering affects those around you? Can you listen deeply, with a caring and honest heart?

and others. And yet, in some way, this busyness was also a way to keep his grief at bay. Finally, when he was ready, he came to a meditation retreat. Somehow he knew that it was time for him to experience his pain directly, to find the cure for the pain in the pain itself. At first, he started his meditations with all of the prayers and mantras and visualizations he had learned. Finally, one morning, he just sat still. As soon as he did, waves of grief and guilt and loss poured out. And the simple and necessary task for healing became evident: to bring a kind attention to all of the grief and suffering from which he could no longer run.

You should never underestimate your power to heal when you step toward difficulty with courage and love, when you touch pain with healing rather than fear. Our healing comes with our own kind attention and through the kind embrace of another. I think of a friend of mine whose teenage daughter had suffered from severe meningitis and was in a rehabilitation hospital. The doctors did not believe she could regain most of her capacities, but this mother sat with her daughter lovingly, day after day for almost a year, picking up her hand and arm and moving it with her, and helping her learn to mouth words one by one. To the doctor's surprise, her daughter recovered. She has now completed law school and practices disability law.

I once observed a great Burmese meditation master who was attending to a young person who had advanced brain cancer and was told she had only months to live. I thought the meditation master would give her instructions on how to die consciously, offering teachings from the great Buddhist texts on making the passage between life and death. Instead, he looked at this young woman and said, "Life is precious. You must do everything you can to heal yourself. Here are some healing prayers, here is healing holy water, here are some healing practices. And, only at the end, if it becomes absolutely clear that you cannot heal yourself, should you let go into the practices for death." This woman dedicated herself to these practices and lived for years longer than anyone expected. As long as you can, find a passion for the preciousness of life, and bring this care to the healing of your heart and body.

Meditation Practice
The Temple of Healing

 This meditation is Track Five on the audio portion of this program.

Sit comfortably and allow your eyes to close. Make sure your seat allows you to be present, awake, grounded, and relaxed. As you sit at ease, feel your connection to the Earth. Center yourself and feel how your breath breathes itself in your body.

Then, without trying to change anything, bring a kind attention to what's comfortable and uncomfortable in your body. Notice if there's tension, contraction, or pain in certain areas, and ease and relaxation in others. Notice if there's clutter in your mind or repetitive thoughts. Notice the state of your heart. Does it feel contracted, or soft and open? Is it full of some emotion or feeling, such as fatigue or joy, sadness or irritation? Simply witness whatever is present without judgment. Breathe and let yourself be easy with it all.

After a few minutes, begin to envision or sense in any way you can that you are floating up into the air as if on a magic carpet, up into the clear, blue sky. Take your time. Feel or imagine or sense that you're floating above the Earth in the stillness of the clear air and luminous sunlight. After a minute or two, allow yourself to gradually descend. Set your intention to descend into a sacred and beautiful Temple of Healing, into a place of great wisdom and healing and love. Let this temple be a surprise. It may be some place you've been before or it may be some place you've never seen. It may be indoors or out. Come to rest in it. Take as much time as you need to imagine and feel and picture this temple.

Now sense how you feel being in this Temple of Healing. What does the energy of this healing place feel like to you? How does it affect your body and spirit to be present there?

As you sense yourself in this temple and feel how its energy is affecting you, let yourself become aware of the wounds you carry that require healing. Once you have at least one injury clearly in mind, become aware that there is a beautiful altar of healing nearby. Now imagine yourself sitting in front of this altar. After a time, a wise and loving healer who lives at this temple will walk toward you. Let yourself open to, sense, or envision this luminous being as they appear. As this healer approaches you, they will bow lightly to you. Next they will put their gentle, healing hand on the part of your body where you are most deeply wounded. Feel the presence of this healing hand on your injured limb, your pained heart, or your wounded brow. If you wish, you can take your own hand and put it on the location of your deepest wound. Hold the place of your sorrow, your difficulty, or your illness. Touch it as if you were guided by this great healing being. Know that no matter how many times you have buried or resisted this injury or sorrow, how many times you've greeted it with fear or aversion, now is the time that you can finally open to it.

As you feel your body opening to this healing touch, explore your sensations. Is the touch warm or cool, hard or soft? Let your awareness be gentle, as if learning the loving touch of Kwan Yin, the goddess of compassion, or Mother Mary, or Jesus. Feel your wounds, fears, and difficulties touched by pure sweetness and openness.

As the very core of your wounds opens to the touch of healing, sense how you've closed off from this pain, how you've wished it would go away, how you've rejected your feelings. Now you are ready to open your heart to experience this pain at last, held by loving attention, with the touch of this luminous being, and by your own hand. Feel the medicine of healing enter you through this touch. Stay with this healing for as long as is helpful. Then shift to any other areas that ask for healing. Take your time.

After this luminous being removes their hand, they have gifts to give you. There is a package of the perfect medicine for you on the altar that this luminous being now places in your hands. This medicine will be in the simple form of a symbol of exactly what you need for healing. Open this gift of medicine and see what is inside the box. If you cannot see it clearly, hold it up to the light. Hold this symbol of the medicine that you need in your hands and become aware of just what it means for you.

Imagine you needed this difficulty to learn a most important lesson. What truth can it teach you?

Now relax and drink in the blessings of being at this healing temple and in the presence of this luminous and wise being. Finally, imagine that they lean over to you with great compassion and whisper into your ear the healing words you most need to hear. Let yourself hear, imagine, think of, or sense the healing words of this being. Receive their blessings in any way you can. Remember their gift and these words and take them into your heart.

Before you leave, if you have any questions for this wise healer, you can ask them and they will answer you. When you feel satisfied, rest in this temple and allow its healing and compassionate spirit to fill your heart and body and mind. Let it touch every part of your being.

Stay as long as you wish. When you are ready to leave, imagine you can bow to this healing being with gratitude for everything they've given to you.

As you depart, know that this temple is inside of you. It is available to return to any time you need it. Remember that you carry all the medicine and healing you will ever need inside your own heart.

CHAPTER SEVEN

The Zen of an Aching Heart

Your days pass like rainbows, like a flash of lightening,
like a star at dawn.
Your life is short. How can you quarrel?

The Buddha

In the Jewish mystical tradition, a great rabbi taught his disciples to memorize and contemplate the teachings and to place the prayers and holy words on their hearts. One day a student asked the rabbi why he always used the phrase "on your heart" and not "in your heart." The master replied, "Only time and grace can put the essence of these stories in your heart. Here we recite and learn them and put them on our hearts hoping that some day when our heart breaks they will fall in."

When your heart breaks—in love, in friendship, in partnership—it is always a very difficult experience. It hurts. Modern neuroscience has discovered that the emotional suffering we experience registers in the same areas of the brain as physical pain. When we're feeling abandoned and rejected, we don't want to eat, we can't sleep, we have difficulty breathing, our bodies feel as if we've been injured, and our hearts ache.

So, what can you do when you are forced to accept the loss of a friend or a lover? What truth can you find beyond the repeated stories we tell ourselves about who's wrong and who's right? What can you do besides spending fruitless hours trying to decipher everything they said or did? Can you do something more useful than justifying to yourself what you said, or wishing

Like a sandcastle, all is temporary. Build it, tend it, enjoy it. And when the time comes, let it go.

that you had done something differently? And what can you do when the story expands to nearly drown you in despair? Or you believe that there's something wrong with you, that you are unlovable, that you're the reason things didn't work out?

The first thing you need to do when you've suffered loss or betrayal is to find a way to regain your dignity and wisdom so you can bear the aching of your heart. The Zen teacher Graf Durckheim speaks of the need to go through our difficulties in a conscious and clear way:

> The man who, being really on the Way, falls upon hard times in the world will not, as a consequence, turn to that friend who offers him refuge and comfort and encourages his old self to survive. Rather, he will seek out someone who will faithfully and inexorably help him to risk himself, so he may endure the suffering and pass courageously through it. Only to the extent that a man exposes himself over and over again to annihilation, can that which is indestructible arise within him. In this lies the dignity of daring.[1]

Sometimes we grow most through suffering, loss, and betrayal. The unexpected breakups that befall us deepen our capacity to lead an authentic and free life. Often by working our way through our difficulties, our ability to love and feel compassion deepens, along with the wisdom that will help us through similar problems in the future. And learning how to survive our own difficulties is one of the few things that will help us to know the right things to say and do when others whom we love suffer as well.

This next meditation invites you to take a seat with your aching, broken heart and to hold it with love and with the dignity and appreciation it deserves.

MEDITATION PRACTICE: ZEN OF AN ACHING HEART

To begin this practice, take a seat and close your eyes. Feel your body seated on the Earth with a deep connection that goes to the core of the Earth.

When you're ready, bring a mindful attention to your broken heart. Feel the ache that's there, and with it any feelings of unworthiness, of longing or fear, of loneliness or vulnerability and neediness. Let yourself feel the tenderness that's there too, alongside any anger or grief, rage or depression. Perhaps you feel abandoned, perhaps you feel confused, perhaps it feels like you're dying.

Now expand your awareness to include your entire body. Is there tightness in your solar plexus? Is there a feeling of emptiness in your chest or belly? Do you feel areas that seem hot or cold? Are there parts of your body that are trembling or shaking? Is there a feeling of pressure in your shoulders? As you become aware of the feelings in your body and heart, continue to sit and hold whatever you become aware of in respectful attention.

Notice too the layers of pain, the stream of old stories of abandonment and loss in your life, your rejections and disappointments. When you feel you can sense all the accumulated pain you've experienced in your life, see if you can visualize it all as a demon that wants to possess you, to injure you, or even to devour you. Then, once you have this image of a demon clearly in your mind, bow to it. We all have our demons, and they too want our respect.

Once you have honored the demon of your pain and broken heart, ask yourself, is this who you really are? Is this pain your essence, your soul? Now open to feel the loneliness that surrounds this wounded heart, a loneliness you share with all living beings, in all times. Then let this loneliness open and expand until it becomes all there is. Feel it change from a personal sense of loneliness to a vast aloneness that is still and silent and permeates the entire world. Then, when you feel that it is complete, breathe gently in this aloneness. Find your peace there. It is your home.

It is where you can come to rest. Breathe in this aloneness gently, and breathe out into the vast space that surrounds you.

Once you feel established within this aloneness, become aware of your cycles in the long history of time, how your life moves with the great turning of the seasons. Look back over your life—first over the last year, then further back over ten, twenty, thirty years. See how many times you have loved and how many times your heart has been broken. You are part of an eternal cycle of joining and separating that you share with all living beings, from all times. Become aware of how many broken hearts there are right now all over the world. Breathe with compassion for them all.

Now, as you sit within this vast perspective, return to your own heart. Listen to what your heart can teach you through its brokenness. It will teach you that through your difficulties you can become strong. It will teach you that by passing through your difficulties you will come to know your true self. By your disappointments and losses you will come to learn who you truly are. You will find what cannot be torn from you, what can't be lost.

Let yourself remember wholeness and well being. From your seat on this Earth connect with a memory of a time when you felt most whole. Breathe in these remembered feelings of wholeness. Again from this wholeness and centeredness, let the songs of all the aching hearts of the world be heard by you. Feel the courage of all of those who are suffering as you do. Breathe together with them and bow to them with compassion and dignity, with love and with tears, with courage and a tender heart.

From the perspective of your vast wisdom, realize that people and things are not possessed by you, they're here for their purpose only. They arrive and pass away, and you can witness them all—the rising and falling—from this wise and understanding perspective. Regardless of your losses, you remain whole.

Place your hand on your broken heart, or your stomach, or your forehead, or wherever you feel the hollowness of your loss. Touch your measure of pain with compassion while simultaneously remembering your dignity and wholeness. Make a vow to be true to your wholeness and let go of everything that makes you feel you are small. Feel that you are—at the deepest level—your own Zen master, and that you see and understand all, and that you can hold it all in your vast, open heart.

True love and faith arrive when it's most dark. In the dark there is a special kind of beauty. In a dark time, your eyes can see your true friends by the light of their lamps.

CHAPTER EIGHT

Equanimity and Peace

Let it be.

Paul McCartney

Mother Theresa was once interviewed for BBC television by Malcolm Muggeridge, and after spending nearly an hour with her as she worked with orphans and those who were dying, he said to her, "You know, this work is so wonderful, Mother Theresa, but in some way, it must be a little bit easier for you as a nun. You have such a simple life, you don't have the complexities of a home, an insurance policy, the difficulties of marriage and relationship." And she interrupted him and said, "No, no, no, I'm married too." And she held up the gold ring that commemorated the wedding of the nuns in her order to Christ. She paused for a moment and then looked up at him and said, "And he can be very difficult sometimes."

If it's true for Mother Theresa, it's true for all of us. We will all experience waves of gain and loss, of fame and disrepute, of praise and blame that wash over us within the vast turnings of life. Each of us has to find our way to keep a peaceful and steady heart in the midst of it all.

To do this, the natural love of the heart has to be balanced with the wisdom of equanimity. If we focus only on feelings of love and compassion without the balance of equanimity and peace, we can get overly attached to the way we want things to be. While we can love the world and hold the sorrows of the world in compassion, we also need equanimity and peace to teach us balance with the things we cannot change.

All the teachings summarized: "Not always so." — Suzuki Roshi

I remember seeing a poster in a health food store in Santa Cruz in the 1970s of the Hindu guru Swami Satchidananda with his long, flowing beard, standing on one leg in a little orange loincloth in the yogic posture called the tree pose. What was remarkable about this picture was that Swami Satchidananda was balanced in the tree pose on top of a surfboard on a really large wave. Underneath, it said in big letters, "You can't stop the waves, but you can learn to surf." The spirit of the practice of equanimity and peace is not that the waves will stop, but that our heart and mind can become so open and balanced, that we can behold the turning seasons of the world from a place of stillness.

To find equanimity and peace requires an acceptance of the mystery of life itself. Modern science tells us that a big bang started the universe, hurling matter through space. Some of this matter formed stars, and some of the residue formed the planets. In this way everything on the Earth—stones, frogs, clouds, and our own living bodies—is formed out of the same material that formed the stars and planets. As the cosmologist Brian Swimme says, "Four and a half billion years ago, the Earth was a flaming molten ball of rock, and now it can sing opera."

When you can appreciate your life as part of this unfolding mystery of the immense forces that formed the entire universe, you can more easily accept the difficulties and hardships that you face. They are part of the unfolding of life. Many of the difficulties you've faced include endings, but none of them so far has been the end of your story. Without knowing the whole story, it is impossible to draw definite conclusions about our difficulties. We are still in the middle of them and don't know how it will all turn out.

Unfortunately, there is no rule book for life. "Things are uncertain, aren't they?" my teacher Ajahn Chah used to say. To accept this basic uncertainty in life is to discover the wisdom of insecurity. When we realize that things are fundamentally uncertain and learn how to relax into this uncertainty, we come to trust in the unfolding of our individual lives within the vastness of all time and space. As Zen master Suzuki Roshi says, "When you realize the truth that everything changes and find your composure in it, you find yourself in Nirvana."

When you lose everything, this is your opportunity to practice courage by standing up for what cannot be lost.

To find composure, it is helpful to reflect on the value of a peaceful heart. "No one can harm you, not even your worst enemy, as much as your own mind untrained. And no one can help you, not even your most loving mother and father, as much as your own mind well trained"—these are the words of Buddha 2,500 years ago, and they echo within us now. When we can train a peaceful heart inside ourselves, we will automatically bring blessings and peace to everything we touch. Zen master Thich Nhat Hanh said that when the crowded Vietnamese refugee boats met with storms or pirates, if everyone on the boat panicked, all was lost. But if even one person on the boat remained calm and centered, it was enough. It showed the way for everyone to survive.

When we can find this same calm center within ourselves, it is as if we reach what is called in bullfighting our *querencia*. The querencia is the place in the ring where the bull feels safe. In order to successfully fight the bull, the matador must force the bull off its querencia, its place of wholeness. This querencia in a human being is our centeredness and balance where—fully aware of our difficulties—we can remain calm, peaceful, and wise. If we can prevent anyone or anything from forcing us out of our querencia, we can gather the strength necessary to accept our difficulties.

It's critical to remember that remaining in our querencia does not require an absence of change or difficulty,
and that the state of peace and equanimity should not
be confused with withdrawal or indifference. Withdrawal
and indifference are called the near enemies to equanimity in Buddhism, which means that they masquerade as
equanimity, but indifference and withdrawal are based
upon fear, not acceptance. True equanimity arises when
we can maintain a sense of balance and openness and
acceptance in the midst of whatever's happening. Equanimity is aware of the vast stillness that surrounds this
changing world. As it says in the *Tao Te Ching*:

*Don't add to the
problem. Don't
add fear. Don't add
confusion. First,
take a breath. Then
simply see the
situation clearly.*

> There's a time for being ahead and a time for being behind, a
> time for being in motion and a time for being at rest, a time for
> being vigorous and a time for being exhausted, a time for being
> in danger and a time to return to safety. The wise one sees things
> as they are without controlling them... They are centered in the
> Tao and can go where they wish without danger, because they
> perceive the harmony, even amidst the joys and sorrows of the
> world. Because they reside at the center of the circle, they have
> found peace in their heart.[1]

With equanimity comes an awareness of the limits of our illusions of control.
We can love and care for others, we can assist them, we can pray for them,
but we cannot control what will happen. Nor can we control the actions or
feelings of our children, our lovers, our friends, or our family. Equanimity
shows us a wiser way to relate to the people in our lives, which is to love them
unconditionally. And acting from this feeling of unconditional love, we can
experience deep feelings of care and concern for them, but know that their
happiness and suffering depend on their actions and not our wishes for them.

It is not within anyone's power to save the whole world, but it is within your power to add whatever you can, with a loving and caring and peaceful heart. You can tend the portion of the world that you touch, you can add a bit of beauty and understanding to the world, you can become the one calm person standing in the boat in a great storm or during an attack by pirates. And by doing so with peace and equanimity, you can show others that it is possible for them to do so as well. When you do, you will join with the forces of peace in the complex unfolding of life. And in that moment you will feel yourself to be one with the vastness from which you and all beings were born, returning to the silence that surrounds you in every moment of your life.

Care, not carelessness, is the way.
—*The Buddha*

Meditation Practice
Equanimity and Peace

 This meditation is Track Six on the audio portion of this program.

Take a seat and find a posture that has ease and dignity. Feel yourself connected to the Earth. Bring a soft attention to your body and feel how your breath breathes itself. Allow your body and mind to settle and to calm more and more with each of the breaths you take.

As you sit quietly, reflect for a moment on the benefit of a mind that has balance and equanimity. You can remember these words from Buddha, when he said, "There are those who discover they can leave behind confused reactions and become patient as the Earth, unmoved by the fires of anger and fear, unshaken as a pillar, unperturbed as a clear and quiet pool." Acknowledge what a great gift it would be to bring a peaceful heart into your own life and into the world around you. Let yourself feel this inner sense of balance and ease. Invite the quality of a peaceful and balanced heart to be here with you. Let it fill your body and mind.

Now, with each breath, let your body and mind become calmer. Invite a great sense of peace to fill you as you gently repeat the simple phrases that follow with each breath. Feel yourself grow calmer as you do.

Breathing in and out, I calm my body.

Breathing in and out, I calm my mind.

May I be balanced.

May I be at peace.

With each breath, gently breathing in and out, I calm my body.

Breathing in and out, I quiet my mind.

May I be balanced and at peace.

Take your time with these phrases. When you start to feel quiet in your body and mind, broaden the sense of calm into a spacious equanimity. Acknowledge that all created things arise and pass away—joys and sorrows, pleasant and painful events, people, buildings, animals, nations, even whole civilizations. Let yourself rest in stillness, a calm and steady witness to this great dance of life.

Now, as you continue to breathe gently, let phrases of equanimity and peace nourish and inspire the true quality of stillness in the midst of all the changes:

May I learn to accept the arising and passing of all things with equanimity and balance.

May I be open and balanced and at peace in the midst of change.

Let stillness enter every part of your being. Let your body and mind open beyond any weariness or struggle, and rest at ease in this vast universe.

Take your time and continue to recite these phrases and invocations of peace. When you feel that you've established a sense of equanimity and peace in yourself, begin to picture the face of a loved one. With them in your mind and heart, repeat these phrases of equanimity and peace:

May you see the arising and passing of all things with equanimity and balance.

May you be open, balanced, and peaceful.

Let the image of this loved one be surrounded by peace. When you feel ready, continue this well-wishing to other loved ones, continuing to breathe gently and mindfully, no matter what arises. And as you reflect on each person, realize that all beings receive the fruit of their own actions. To free your heart from their struggles and to love them with equanimity and peace, add these additional equanimity phrases:

Your happiness and suffering depend on your actions and not my wishes for you.

May you find openness and balance and peace.

As the quality of equanimity and peace grows in you, you can gradually expand the meditation to include loved ones, friends, neighbors, and benefactors. Picture each one in turn, and recite inwardly the phrases of equanimity as a blessing of peace.

Next expand the circle of the blessings of peace to include people you don't know, and animals, and all living things, and finally the whole of the Earth. As you develop the practice of equanimity further, you can include the difficult people in your life—even the most difficult—wishing that they too find equanimity and peace.

Finally, bring your attention back to yourself, seated on the Earth with a peaceful heart, and repeat:

May I see the arising and passing of all with equanimity and balance.

May I be open and balanced, may my heart be at peace.

Your happiness and suffering depend on your actions and not my wishes for you.

May I and all beings rest with a peaceful heart,

May we find balance and peace, compassion and equanimity, amidst all things of this world.

In hard times when you get distracted and reactive, stop. Breathe. Invite mindfulness. Mindfulness sees kindly, without reacting. You know how.

Continue equanimity practice as long as you like, resting in the heart of great peace.

When you get up from this equanimity practice, look around at your environment and the world you've created around you. Determine to make your home a zone of peace. Turn off CNN or Fox News and turn on Mozart. Open the curtains and walk in the hills. Plant a garden and then sit in it while the birds come and go. Make time to reconnect to the great seasons of life and be the still point in the center of them all.

CHAPTER NINE

Your Highest Intention

Live in joy, even among the troubled.

The Buddha

Every morning when the Dalai Lama wakes up, he begins his morning practices with a prayer from Shantideva: "May I be a guard for those who need protection; a guide for those on the path; a boat, a raft, a bridge for those to cross the flood; may I be a lamp in the darkness; a resting place for the weary, and a healing medicine for all who are sick. For as long as Earth and sky endure, may I assist until all living beings are awakened." This is the Dalai Lama's way of reaffirming the direction of his life and the direction of his heart before he starts his day. With this powerful prayer, the Dalai Lama recites his vow of compassion and love for all beings, even in the face of the great difficulties of the Tibetan people.

You too need a reliable compass to set your direction and steer through the rough waters. When you are going through hard times, when you've been betrayed, when you've lost your job, when you've lost your friends or loved ones, when you're in conflict with your family, or when you're going through illness, you need a way to guide yourself.

But how can you set your direction when you can't see any clear harbor? And how can you navigate through difficult waters when you're swamped by overwhelming emotions, when so much of your awareness is taken over with trying to figure out who's at fault and who did what to whom, or creating stories about who's wrong and who's right and why? When we're overwhelmed by a difficult situation, sometimes we know we're behaving in a way that is only making matters worse, but we don't know how to stop.

Simplicity, whether chosen or forced upon us, is still a gift.

Yet even though a part of us may be grieving or angry or wanting revenge, there is a wiser spirit in us that knows that it would be best for everyone involved if we behaved with dignity and courage and magnanimity, no matter what the circumstances.

In the Buddhist tradition, one who dedicates themselves to the spirit of courage and compassion is called a *bodhisattva*. *Bodhi* means awakened, and *sattva* means being. A bodhisattva is a being committed to the awakening of the good heart in everyone. A bodhisattva is committed to compassion, committed to making known the shining beauty that is possible for the human spirit, not because they believe that it is somehow a "better" way to live but because they know that it is the only way to be fully alive and awake.

As I write these words, Nobel Prize winner Aung San Suu Kyi, leader of the democracy movement in Burma, has just been released from house arrest after almost seventeen years. She's a small woman at sixty-five, just my age, well-educated and thoughtful. During her confinement, the Burmese military dictatorship told her that she was free to leave the country at any time, but that if she left she could never return. She desperately wanted to be with her husband in England as he lay dying of cancer, and to be with her children when they graduated from university, but she decided she could not leave her people. She remained in Burma under house arrest as a symbol of freedom for the fifty million oppressed Burmese. Through all these years her position was, "I will not leave Burma. And I will not hate you." By remaining under house arrest because of her commitment to the people of Burma and to the country she loves, she demonstrated a spirit of dedication and fearlessness, showing everyone else what is possible. As I've traveled around Burma, no one dares to speak openly of Aung San Suu Kyi for fear of government spies and reprisals. Even when I ask them in private, they cover their lips with their hands as if to say, "We may not speak." But then they put their hands on their hearts and whisper, "She is always here with us." This one small person carries the flame of freedom for millions of others.

A spoon of salt in a cup tastes salty. A spoon of salt in a lake, and the water tastes pure. Open up. Look at the sky. See the big picture.

Living our highest intentions can happen in great ways, such as in the work of Aung San Suu Kyi, or in what may seem small—yet critical—ways of refusing to be conquered by the difficulties that come to us in our lives. We can choose our spirit in spite of everything. Sometimes, all we'll be able to offer is a smile to the weary or forlorn on the streets. Sometimes it will be to plant a garden where there was none, or plant seeds of patience in a family or of reconciliation in community difficulty. No matter what situation we find ourselves in, we can always set our compass to our highest intentions in the present moment. Perhaps it is nothing more than being in a heated conversation with another person and stopping to take a breath and asking yourself, "What is my highest intention in this moment?" If you have enough awareness to take this small step, your heart will give you an answer that will take the conversation in a different, more positive direction. Or before you enter a room to speak with those with whom you are in conflict, you can pause, take a breath, and ask yourself, "What is my highest intention in this situation?" With simple steps like these, you can behave in ways that at least will not fuel your difficulties—or anyone else's. As Albert Camus wrote, "We all carry within us our places of exile, our crimes, our ravages. But our task is not to unleash them on the world; it is to fight them in ourselves and others."

When your thoughts are racing and repetitive, remember: no one can harm you as much as your untamed mind. When you are struggling or in pain remember: no one can help you as much as a quiet, clear, composed mind.

When you're overwhelmed by illness or loss, by the conflicts around you, when you feel you are lost in the darkness, sometimes all you can do is to breathe consciously and gently with your pain and anguish and know that with this simple gesture you are resetting the compass of your heart, no matter your circumstances. By taking that one simple, mindful breath, you will return again to compassion and realize that you are more than your fears and confusions.

Whatever your difficulties—a devastated heart, financial loss, feeling assaulted by the conflicts around you, or a seemingly hopeless illness—you can always remember that you are free in every moment to set the compass of your heart to your highest intentions. You can offer the best of yourself in any circumstance, including in difficult times. In fact, the two things that you are always free to do—despite your circumstances—are to be present and to be willing to love.

It's important to remember that you mustn't expect everyone to respond to your efforts. The point isn't to completely change everything immediately. If you set your highest intention to compassion and courage and truth, it doesn't really matter if you see an immediate effect or not. The Christian mystic Thomas Merton wrote to a young activist, "Do not depend on the hope of results. . . You may have to face the fact that your work will be apparently worthless and even achieve no result at all, if not perhaps results opposite to what you expect. As you get used to this idea, you start more and more to concentrate not on the results but on the value, the rightness, the truth of the work itself."[1]

This means that sometimes you may be able to improve a situation immediately, and that sometimes you will have to steadily carry the lamp for yourself and others through a period of darkness. Your intuition and your good heart will guide the way.

MEDITATION PRACTICE: YOUR HIGHEST INTENTION

In this practice, take a seat where you feel grounded and at ease. Be seated with dignity, halfway between heaven and Earth. Allow your eyes to close, and take a few breaths to center yourself.

As you become quiet, let yourself reflect upon an inspiring person—someone you know or have seen or read about, someone whose life inspires the best in you. It could be that lone man with the shopping bags in front of the tanks at Tiananmen Square. It could be the mothers in Argentina who came out every day to demonstrate against the dictatorship, no matter what happened to them. It could be Nelson Mandela walking out of Robben Island Prison after twenty-seven years, with his graciousness and compassion intact. It could be the Dalai Lama or a grandmother you know, or a doctor or health-care worker, a dedicated teacher, a friend.

As you visualize this inspiring being, imagine you can sense their presence, or hear their voice. In some way let them come alive to you, and feel their spirit present with you. Feel your connection to them. Recognize that the spirit of courage, compassion, and magnanimity that you admire in them is the same spirit that can be found in your own heart as well. And as you sit quietly, sense how this connection with the one you admire reflects on the bodhisattva spirit that resides within you too.

As you do, begin to allow the wisest voice inside you—whether it's the still small voice or the lion's roar—to speak to you from the deep reaches of your heart. Let the message you hear be your highest intention. Know that in the difficulties where you find yourself now, in the midst of your struggle and pain, this voice of wisdom can set the compass of your heart to its highest intention.

Now continue to listen to this deepest part of your heart and make a vow, whatever speaks your highest truth in this moment. Say, *"I vow in the midst of my difficulties to…"* and listen for your answer. It may be as simple as, *"I vow to remain kind no matter what."* Or, *"I vow to be true to myself."* Or to be dignified

Visualize the best outcome possible in this hard situation. Keep focused on your creative responses. Know your highest intentions. Write them down. Remember them.

and respectful to all. Listen for your own vow. Reflect on this vow until you come to realize what gifts it holds for you. Know that you have carried the lamp of this vow in you, that this has always been your highest intention, no matter how many times you've stumbled, how many times you've been overwhelmed or confused. And know that you will continue to carry this vow with you no matter the circumstances. Know that you cannot help but carry this lamp because its light is your source, and you are the lamp. Know that you can always remember it, reaffirm it, and return to it whenever you feel lost or are struggling in the darkness. And feel your kinship with the inspired being who helped you to remember your vow, who you really are. This being is a visual reminder of what you yourself are as well. Inwardly thank them, bow to the qualities of their life that are reflected in yours. Know that this is how you can live from now on. And by carrying the lamp of your highest intention, know that your lamp will shine onto others, illuminating the one heart that we all share.

Continue to sit quietly and sense how you can carry the lamp of this vow back into the situation of your difficulty. Let it illuminate and guide you. When you feel ready, open your eyes and find a piece of paper and write your vow on it. Take this paper and place it somewhere where you will see it regularly, so that you can remember it and honor it when you've forgotten. And remember that you do not simply carry the lamp; you yourself are the lamp. Carry it so that you and others see with clarity and compassion even in the deepest darkness.

CHAPTER TEN

The Four Foundations of Mindfulness and the Healing Journey

The meditation instructions for mindfulness given by Buddha begin with a joyful invitation: there is a wonderful way for living beings to overcome grief and sorrow, to end pain and anxiety, to travel the path of compassion and understanding, to realize liberation. And this way is the establishment of mindfulness. Mindfulness is a balanced, kind, non-judging attention. With mindfulness we can see clearly, free ourselves from reactivity, and respond wisely.

The Buddha goes on: mindfulness is to be established in four ways. We must establish mindfulness of the body in the body, mindfulness of the feelings in the feelings, mindfulness of the mind in the mind, and mindfulness of the dharma (the laws that govern life), in the dharma. Mindfulness leads to healing and the end of sorrow and grief. Mindfulness brings liberation.

So, how does the healing of our bodies, our emotions, and our mind grow out of mindfulness? Healing comes from our innate capacity for deep listening. Zen master Thich Nhat Hanh also calls it "looking deeply." This deep listening or seeing is not through our ears or our eyes, but with our heart and our soul.

Mindfulness is the means by which we can bring our full presence to the world and, with balance and understanding, experience its ten thousand joys and sorrows. The open attention of mindfulness liberates us from reacting to and being caught by all things in the world.

Recently, I experienced some significant neurological problems. After my Western doctors couldn't find a cause, I went to see Dr. Yeshi Dhonden, longtime physician to the Dalai Lama. I remembered how Richard Selzer, a surgeon at Yale, described the first time he saw Yeshi Dhonden diagnose a patient in his hospital:

> On the bulletin board in the front hall of the hospital where I work there appeared an announcement: "Yeshi Dhonden will make rounds at six o'clock on the morning of June 10." The particulars were then given, followed by a notation: "Yeshi Dhonden is Personal Physician to the Dalai Lama." I'm not so leathery a skeptic that I would knowingly ignore an emissary from the gods. . . Thus, on the morning of June 10, I join the clutch of whitecoats waiting in the small conference room. . . The air in the room is heavy with ill-concealed dubiety and suspicion of bamboozlement. At precisely six o'clock, he materializes, a short, golden, barrelly man dressed in a sleeveless robe of saffron. . . His scalp is shaven, and the only visible hair is a scanty black line above each hooded eye.

> He bows in greeting while his young interpreter makes the introduction. Yeshi Dhonden, we are told, will examine a patient selected by a member of the staff. The diagnosis is as unknown to Yeshi Dhonden as it is to us. [It] will take place in our presence; afterward, we will meet and discuss his diagnosis. We are further informed that for the past few hours, Yeshi Dhonden has purified himself by bathing, fasting, and praying. I, having breakfasted well, performed only the most desultory of ablutions, and [gave] no thought at all to my soul. I glance furtively at my fellows. Suddenly, we seem a soiled, uncouth lot.

> The patient [was] awakened early and told that she was to be examined by a foreign doctor, and she had been asked to produce a

fresh specimen of urine, so when we enter her room, the woman shows no surprise. She has long ago taken on that mixture of compliance and resignation that is the face of chronic illness. This was to be but another in an endless series of tests and examinations. Yeshi Dhonden steps to the bedside while the rest [of us] stand apart, watching. For a long time he gazes at the woman, favoring no part of her body with his eyes, but seeming to fix his glance at a place just above her supine form. I too study her. No physical sign or symptom gives a clue to the nature of her disease.

At last he takes her hand, raising it in both of his own. Now he bends over the bed in a kind of crouching stance, his head drawn down into the collar of his robe. His eyes are closed as he feels for her pulse. In a moment he has found the spot, and for the next half hour he remains thus suspended above the patient like some exotic golden bird with folded wings, holding the pulse of the woman beneath his fingers, cradling her hand in his. All the power of the man seems to have been drawn down . . . into the palpation of the pulse. . .From where I stand, it is as though he and the patient have entered a special place of isolation, of apartness, about which. . . no violation is possible. After a moment, the woman rests back upon her pillow. From time to time, she raises her head to look at the strange figure above her and then sinks back once more. I cannot see their hands joined in a correspondence that is exclusive, intimate—his fingertips receiving the voice of her sick body through the rhythm and throb she offers at her wrist. All at once I am envious—not of him, not of Yeshi Dhonden for his gift of beauty and holiness, but of her. I want to be held like that, touched so, *received*. And I know that I, who have palpated a hundred-thousand pulses, have not felt a single one.

At last, Yeshi Dhonden straightens, gently places the woman's hand upon the bed, and steps back. The interpreter produces a small wooden bowl and two sticks. Yeshi Dhonden pours a portion of the urine specimen into the bowl and proceeds to whip the liquid. . . for several minutes until the foam is raised. Then bowing above the bowl, he inhales the odor three times. He sets down the bowl and turns to leave. All this while, he has not uttered a single word. As he nears the door, the woman raises her head and calls out to him in a voice at once urgent and serene. "Thank you, doctor," she says, and touches with her other hand the place he had held on her wrist, as though to recapture something that had visited her there. Yeshi Dhonden turns back for a moment to gaze at her, then steps into the corridor. Rounds are at an end.

We are seated once more in the conference room. Yeshi Dhonden speaks now for the first time, in soft Tibetan sounds that I have never heard before. He has barely begun when the young interpreter begins to translate, the two voices continuing in tandem—a bilingual fugue, the one chasing the other. It is like the chanting of monks. He speaks of winds coursing through the body of the woman, currents that break against barriers, eddying. These vortices are in her blood, he says. The last spendings of an imperfect heart. Between the chambers of her heart, long, long before she was born, a wind had come and blown open a deep gate that must never be opened. Through it charge the full waters of her river, as the mountain stream cascades in the springtime, battering, knocking loose the land, and flooding her breath. Thus he speaks and is silent.

"May we now have the diagnosis?" the professor asks. The host of these rounds, the man who knows, answers. "Congenital heart disease," he says. "Interventricular septal defect with resultant heart failure."

A gateway in the heart, I think. [One] that must not be opened. Through it charge the full waters that flood her breath. So! Here then is the doctor listening to the sounds of the body to which the rest of us are deaf. He is more than doctor. He is priest.

I know. . . the doctor to the gods is pure knowledge, pure healing. The doctor to man stumbles; his patients must die, as must he.

Now and then it happens, as I make my own rounds, that I hear the sound of [Yeshi Dhonden's] voice, like an ancient Buddhist prayer, its meaning long since forgotten, only the music remaining. Then a jubilation possesses me, and I feel myself as if touched by something divine.[1]

I had never met Yeshi Dhonden before I went to visit him in Oakland this year. He's in his eighties now, and he felt my pulse and did an entire examination. After reading Dr. Selzer's account, I had a lot of expectations. As I came into his presence I can recall the same longing to be so held, to be so received, so listened to, so respected. After hearing my story, he slowly and carefully read my pulse. Then he looked at me long and thoroughly. To foster healing, he gave me some Tibetan medicine to eat, pills that looked like deer pellets. Finally he gave me a beautiful blessing and told me I would get well. I was so happy I saw him.

We all have the same longing to be respected and listened to and held. Whether the Afghanis or the Pakistanis, the Jews, the Muslims, or the Christians, the prisoners and their guards, your co-workers and managers, your children and your parents, and the laborers who harvest the food you eat. Who doesn't want to be listened to with respect? If you look at the people in your life, it will only take you a moment to realize who of the people you know really needs to be deeply listened to right now.

This story of Yeshi Dhonden taking a single pulse tells us of the power of the listening heart. In the face of suffering and illness, and the impermanence of everything we love, this quality of listening allows us to discover the path of healing, to find the way through our present difficulties.

I remember being with a very close friend of mine who was dying of cancer. The intravenous chemotherapy she was doing every other day was so intense that she described it as a combination of fire and hell in her body. And so we practiced the visualization of "The Temple of Healing" together. From this, she realized that she could go through the chemotherapy as if she was at a temple going through a purifying fire, and this visualization became her meditation for that period of time. As she reinterpreted her situation into one of going through a purifying fire, she felt her pain and suffering transform into something positive. Gradually she saw a beautiful green spiritual light come out of the fire as if someone had thrown copper into it. And at that moment she knew that sometimes we have to go right into the fire in order to find our true healing.

When we listen as Yeshi Dhonden did, we learn to trust the capacity of our heart to face the exact reality that is in front of us. And that reality will include the sorrow of a woman with a terminal illness in her hospital bed, and the unbearable beauty of the lavender sunset and luminous maple leaves outside her window. Our listening heart has the ability to acknowledge the way the world is. It knows that life is just like this.

As we learn to listen in this way, we can rest in awareness itself. Mindful presence has respect and care in it. It is a spacious and sacred attention. There's an alchemy that happens when we listen in this way that transforms the struggles and difficulties of the moment into something larger.

We become aware of everything—our joys and sorrows, the relationships between ourselves and others—with a calm mind and open heart.

As Lauren Slater explains, "In this time of managed care [in our medical practices], more emphasis seems to be placed upon medication and the quick amelioration of symptoms short-term work and privatized, profit-making clinics, than upon the lovely and mysterious alchemy that comprises the [healing] chords between people, the chords that can soothe some terrors and help us heal."[2]

When we're sick, we are fortunate to benefit from the skills of our modern medical establishment. But there's another level of healing that's much deeper. The philosopher Voltaire once explained, "The art of medicine primarily consists of amusing the patient while nature cures the disease." In truth, much of modern medicine offers ways to get rid of impurities and pathogens, which then gives the body and its life force the opportunity to heal itself.

MINDFULNESS OF THE BODY

So how do the four foundations of mindfulness as the gateway to liberation become a healing path through difficult times? Remember, the Buddha's instruction begins with the phrase, "Be mindful of the body in the body." To start with, bring mindfulness to your human incarnation. You will become aware of your body as a peculiar physical form with four limbs and little wiggly cylinders with remnants of claws at the ends of your feet and hands. There are patches of fur, and a hole at one end in which you regularly stuff plants and animals, grind them up, and then swallow them into a long tube that takes out the nutrients and pushes everything you can't use out the other end. If you look closely at the way you ambulate, you fall forward to one side and then catch yourself, and then fall to the other side and catch yourself again. And somewhere arising with this bizarre form is the sense of "you"— feeling as if you're stuck somewhere in there. It is a mystery, being born into a human body.

Without mindfulness, you take your body for granted, or ignore the body as if it's not important. James Joyce described this relationship in the line, "Mr. Duffy lived a short distance from his body." Or you can fall into the other extreme of clinging and fear and overidentification with this body. You can try to control its appearance with cosmetics and use Botox and exercise and diet to keep it looking good. It's fine to care for the body, but it's also possible that the wrong kind of attention will lead you into unhealthy fears and attachments about how your body should look.

Buddha's invitation for healing is to come into a mindful relationship with the body in our own body. You must start with attention to what your actual experience of being in this body is here and now.

When you sit down to meditate, you might expect to become peaceful and quiet, but often the first thing you actually experience is tightness and pain in the sensations of your body. You become aware of all the tensions you are carrying. If you've been busy running around or you've experienced a period of difficulties, as you slow down and become mindful, you'll probably first become aware of everything that you've been ignoring in your body. You may notice that your jaw is tight, or there's discomfort in your back, or that there's tension in your shoulders, or there's some other pain in your body that calls for your attention. At first it might seem that you'll never get beyond these pains and troubles you carry around with you all day long. But as you learn to meditate, your perspective grows and you become aware that being in a body is sometimes painful and sometimes pleasant. Sometimes you experience tingling or heat or cold or pain and sometimes you feel a release of the tension that was there.

The important question is, can you touch the difficulties in your body with mindfulness? Do you ignore your body and convince yourself that your physical body doesn't matter? Do you react against what is unpleasant? Do you continually struggle to fix it? Do you hate the way your body feels or looks? Do you fear it as it ages and brings you pain?

The problem with trying to fix your body is the inevitability of aging and death. Whatever you do to make yourself comfortable or beautiful, it keeps changing. When you're cold you turn up the heat until you're warm. But soon you're turning it down because you've become too hot. There is no end to this.

Healing starts by simply becoming mindful of the body as it is. To be mindful is to touch the body with benevolent attention, to acknowledge it, to say yes to this mysterious human body that you've been given. One Catholic priest explained it this way:

> I came from a poor, white family where we drank and lived hard. The men treated the body like a truck that you used and ignored. After I joined the church, it got worse. I hated to deal with my body. I lived on coffee and then on scotch. Gradually, as I looked at the simple people who came to talk to me and saw how many tortured bodies there were, as well as tortured souls, my faith and love got past all the nonsense about the sinfulness of the body in church. It doesn't have to be so hard. Christ taught us to love the enemy, so I took a vow of nonviolence and this included my body. My practice became "do not torment myself, do not escalate the pain. Let me touch the body with the same reverence I would touch that which is holy."[3]

When things get difficult, pay benevolent attention to your body. Do this the same way you hold a child who is ill. As any parent knows, when your child is sick, you give the baby medicine and sometimes she continues to cry, so you hold her until the medicine takes effect. In the same way you can hold what is difficult in your body like a sick child with kind attention. As you do, often the places that are wounded start to open up, and the body's healing energy begins to flow back into the areas of pain and discomfort.

So the first step of healing comes from attention itself, the deep healing that comes from being held. As our attention and mindfulness grow, compassion naturally arises. With mindfulness and compassion together we can begin to listen more deeply—the way Yeshi Dhonden listens.

This deep listening begins the second phase of healing. Through listening deeply, you understand what is happening with your body. With a compassionate attention, the body restores its strength, life force, and resiliency. It also teaches us that these are balanced with its vulnerability, its illnesses and aging, and its inevitable death. No matter what is happening, we realize that living in our body is only a temporary condition. Consciousness knows that it is not the body. It sees, "Oh, the body's gotten older, it's gotten droopier," but it knows that the body is not who you are. Your body does not belong to you. You rent it for a while, like a car or hotel room, but it's not your true home. Still, it's the only body you have in this incarnation, so you naturally want to take good care of it.

Knowing that you are not your body, that it's a vehicle for you with vulnerabilities and preciousness, brings compassion. You offer a healing to your body. You become aware of everything you're doing that affects it. You begin to bring mindfulness to what you're putting into your body: instead of just putting something into your mouth out of habit, you consider whether you should be eating this food or not. You sense what is healthy for you, what kind of exercise you need, the benefits of a simpler diet, the appropriate amount of rest and exertion you need each day. As you listen with love, your body will teach you everything you need to know to heal and live wisely.

You can do this even now. Reflect for a moment on how you have listened to your body in the past. Then reflect on your body right this minute—

in whatever condition it's in—with compassionate attention. What kind of attention does it want? What would best honor its strength and life force? What would boost its resilience and well-being? What healing truth is your body trying to teach you right now?

When you listen to your body in this way, you can also feel that it's the Earth's body. Its bones are made of Earth minerals, calcium and magnesium, and there is seawater in your blood. Your body is winter wheat and asparagus and French brie and everything you eat. It's not just your body but part of something bigger: you are the Earth come alive.

Listening deeply, your body will connect you back to the body of the Earth. As you sense that you are not separate from the planet, you know that to take care of your body you also must take care of the streams and the rivers, and the web of life within which you exist. "What is man," said Chief Seattle, "without the beasts? If all the beasts were gone, man would die from great loneliness of spirit, for whatever happens to the beasts also happens to man." Chief Seattle spoke these words 150 years ago, and they bring tears today because they're more true today than ever. You live within the same wheel of nature as the endangered species: the elephant, the black rhinoceros, the Siberian tiger, the threatened species of whales and cranes and frogs. Without mindful attention, you can fail to understand your personal connection to all living things.

So the healing that comes from paying attention to our own mysterious body leads directly to an understanding of our connection to the body of Earth. Mindfulness of the body means developing awareness of who we truly are.

MINDFULNESS OF FEELINGS

The second foundation of mindfulness is awareness of feelings in the feelings. This is a critical foundation, because much of the insanity in the world comes from people not knowing what to do with their feelings. We are nuclear giants and emotional infants.

Feelings are ever-present. With mindfulness, you discover that all experience is colored by three primary feelings: pleasant, neutral, and unpleasant. And from these primary feelings grow a plethora of secondary emotions. Without mindfulness, you react automatically to these primary feelings, habitually clinging to the pleasant ones, avoiding the unpleasant ones, and remaining unaware of what is neutral to us. This constant reactiveness limits your ability to find balance and clarity in your daily life, and limits your ability to love.

"The most difficult part about the sorcerer's way," says Castaneda's Don Juan, "is the realization that the world is a feeling." This is a mysterious statement, but what kind of healing and liberation would be possible without an awareness of the relationship between our feelings and the world? Just as there is healing and liberation of the body, there is a similar healing and liberation possible with our feelings and emotions.

It helps to realize the importance of emotions in all that we believe. Justice William O. Douglas of the Supreme Court has written, "We who work at the Supreme Court level, where I do, understand that 90 percent of our decisions are made on an emotional basis; the other 10 percent supplies the rationality for those decisions." That doesn't just apply to Supreme Court justices, of course. With mindfulness, we realize how the same principle operates in our personal lives.

Many years ago I copied part of a list of five hundred feelings from a psychological textbook. They include affectionate, ambitious, aggressive, ambivalent, angry, amused, amorous, agitated, amazed, antagonistic, antsy, apathetic, apoplectic, appreciative, argumentative, apprehensive, awed, alarmed, blissful, brave, bewildered, bitter, brokenhearted, bored, bonkers, burdened, bubbly, bad, calm, cheerful, claustrophobic, concentrated, cranky, courageous, contracted, curious, concerned, compassionate, certain, content, defiant, delighted, depressed, disheartened, disillusioned, desirous, driven, dull, distressed, disappointed. These are just some of the feelings listed. You and everyone you've met have had all of these feelings.

So how do we bring mindfulness to feelings? The first step is to know the feelings in themselves, just as the first step in mindfulness of the body begins with becoming aware of the body. Just as you have a body but you are not your body, feelings have their own life and need to be known for what they are. You can begin simply with an awareness of pain as pain, of sadness as sadness. You name them: this is joy, this is excitement, this is fear, this is contentment. Just as when you look in a mirror you become aware of your body from the perspective of mindful awareness, you can become aware of your feelings as they rise and fall. With awareness you see that feelings are not who you really are, that you are not your emotions. Instead you see that the everchanging feelings and emotions are simply part of the dance of life that you can hold with appreciation and wisdom.

What you learn from bringing mindfulness to your emotions is that the emotions themselves are not the problem: your difficulties come from your relationship to them. At times Buddhist teaching emphasizes the importance of paying attention to difficult emotions such as greed, hatred, jealousy, and fear, because they are the roots of most suffering. But focusing on difficult emotions alone can become one-sided. The poet William Blake offers a more balanced relation to emotions:

> *It is right it should be so*
> *Man was made for joy and woe*
> *And when this we rightly know*
> *Through the world we safely go.*
> *Joy and woe are woven fine*
> *A clothing for the soul divine*
> *And under every grief and pine*
> *Runs a joy with silken twine*
> *—from "Auguries of Innocence"*

In this vision, Blake saw that joy and sorrow are woven together; you can't have one without the other. You can't have birth without death, or pleasure without pain, or hot without cold, nor light without dark. Our feelings and emotions of joy and sorrow are ever-changing, like a river.

If you're not aware of your emotions, you can become lost in them or frightened of them. But if you can create enough space to hold them with mindfulness and wisdom, you can see how they represent an important part of the picture, but not the entirety of the truth. You can see that anger has some truth in it, but it also has some delusion in it. And when you see love clearly, you can see that often love has some truth in it and that it also has some delusion. You can learn to become mindful of the river of emotions, just as we became aware of the river of sensations in the body, knowing that we are not limited by what is arising in the river.

At first, just as you can become overwhelmed by sensations in the body, you can feel overwhelmed by strong emotions, especially those arising from unfinished business in the heart. When you practice mindful attention or sit in meditation, whatever is unfinished in you will arise. With a little space and quiet, what you've been avoiding comes out to be tended. It may be love or longing, conflict or desire. If you've been avoiding mourning a relationship that you've lost, you will become aware of the grief you carry for the relationship that's ended. Mindfulness becomes the means for you to fully and deeply grieve. The Urdu poet Ghalib explains:

> *For the raindrop, joy is in entering the river . . .*
> *Travel far enough into sorrow, tears turn into sighing . . .*
> *When after heavy rains the stormclouds disperse,*
> *is it not true they've wept themselves clear to the end?*[4]

Sometimes you weep for your own sorrows, and sometimes for the suffering of others. Sometimes you weep for the state of the world around you. To open to tears is to return to the world through the door of compassion.

During our retreats with young men from inner-city gangs, at first they just sit there, dubious about meditation, poetry, and ritual. But if we begin by creating an altar with a table and a candle, everything changes. We simply ask these guys to go out to the stream or the parking lot and find a stone for every young person they know who has died and put it on the altar. And when they put the stone on the altar, we ask them to say the name of their dead friend aloud. In ten minutes, some of these guys come back with their hands full of stones, more stones than you can imagine. As they put them on the altar and they say, "This one is for Jose, this one is for Keela, this is for Tiny," and it just goes on and on—a litany of those who have died too soon. By the time the altar has their stones piled on it, we have all come into the room together—the living and the dead—and the room has become a kind of shrine, a holy place. Once we've shared this experience of building the altar to all the dead who can't be there with us in the flesh but are among us in spirit, we can begin a real conversation, about the sorrows that these young people carry with them that are too heavy for anyone to carry, especially our youth. Something holy happens when we're strong enough to turn and face the tears that we've held inside. It creates a space inside us that we can honorably fill with joy, once our tears have been wept out completely.

In *Black Elk Speaks,* the autobiography of one of the greatest Native American medicine men as told through his conversations with John Neihardt, Black Elk tells about the great visions he had of the whole world while on Harney Peak in the Dakotas. He saw a sacred hoop that contained room for all people to live in harmony, and he believed that this vision was sent to him so that he could save his tribe and their homeland from the destruction brought by soldiers and settlers. But at the end of his life, after all of his work to fulfill this vision, Black Elk felt he had failed and that the sacred hoop was irrevocably broken.

In the last chapter of the book, Black Elk tells Neihardt that he wants to take one final hike up Harney Peak. The Sioux holy man explains that when death approaches, a Lakota will climb this mountain to see if the Great Spirit approves of their life. And rain will fall as a blessing on those who have the Great Spirit's approval. So one clear summer morning, the old man dressed himself in red long johns, moccasins, war paint, and a feathered war headdress. Slowly and laboriously, he climbed to the summit, oblivious of the tourists who stared at him. Neihardt teased him that he should have picked a day with at least one rain cloud in the sky, but Black Elk dismissed him, saying that the rain would have nothing to do with the weather. At the top of the peak, not far from all the tourists, the old man lay down under a blue sky. And, to his astonishment, Neihardt watched as a few small clouds immediately formed over Black Elk and a soft rain began to fall. Black Elk wept with relief, saying he felt that even though he hadn't succeeded in fulfilling his vision, the Great Spirit was signaling that he had done his best.

We don't have to wait until the end of our lives for those tears to come. There's a grace that comes when we're willing to touch the full measure of our feelings, of fear and longing and failure and great love that's inside every one of us. And then all the impediments remain inside us and the frozen emotions become a source of real healing. When we allow our feelings to be met in the space of awareness, where they can arrive and go, we become free. Mindfulness of the feelings inside the feelings liberates them by receiving them spaciously, as the Buddha within who knows, "Ah, this too."

MINDFULNESS OF THE MIND

The third foundation is mindfulness of the mind in the mind. "Who is your enemy?" asks Buddha. "Mind is your enemy. No one can harm you more than your own mind untamed. And who is your friend? Mind is your friend. No one can help you more than your own mind, wisely trained—not even your own mother and father."

How can we be mindful of the mind in the mind? Just as there's a river of bodily sensations passing through consciousness, just as there's a river of five hundred emotions passing through us, there's also a river of thoughts. If you try to sit silently for a minute, what happens? Does your mind become quiet and stay quiet? The mind will not become quiet upon command. Instead, what most people experience is the inner waterfall, a cascading stream of thoughts. It's like a cartoon I saw once of a car crossing the vast landscape of the Utah desert, where a roadside sign says, "Your own tedious thoughts the next 200 miles."

One scientist declared that we have an average of about 67,000 thoughts a day. I think it's probably closer to 37,000, but whatever the number is, the river of thoughts are not under your control. And these thoughts have very little honesty. They will tell you any kind of story, and be dedicated to many beliefs that are absurd. Much of the river is composed of reruns. It's like not being able to sleep in a hotel room and you pick up the remote control and turn on the TV but all you can get are the cable shopping stations selling cheap jewelry and gimmicky kitchen gadgets with a breathless sense of urgency that just goes on and on. But in your case, it's reruns of your last love affair or of a conversation you had at work, or anxiety and shame about some problem, or anger at being treated poorly by someone in your distant past. And no matter what you wish, you have trouble changing the channel. The whole parade just keeps repeating and repeating without resolution. It can be really crazy in there—have you noticed?

What can you do with your thoughts, especially the stories of anxiety and fear? As Michel de Montaigne said, "My life has been filled with terrible misfortunes. Most of which never happened." With mindfulness of the mind, you come to realize that much of what you believe is the product of your imagination. Thoughts can be misleading in many ways. Your thoughts are filled with praise and blame, hope and fear. You will hear the voices of your parents, internalized like monologues, sometimes appearing as the inner judge and the inner tyrant. Then are the voices of the unloved child or the ambitious achiever, voices who are always trying to fix or deceive us. There are healthy voices, wise voices, and loving voices, too. But most of the time your thoughts are like a bureaucracy that continues to perpetuate itself even when the need for it has been outgrown, even when it's actually become unpleasant and restrictive and possibly dangerous to you. Marcus Aurelius wrote, "The soul becomes dyed with the color of its thoughts." So what can you do?

With mindfulness, you can stop taking them so seriously. You can come to know that your thoughts make a good servant but not a good master. You can step back and listen to your thoughts mindfully and then decide whether they're useful or not. It's true that you still need some thoughts to plan for the future, and to problem-solve, but you could eliminate 90 percent of your thoughts and still have plenty to do the job.

So the first thing you can do is to listen to your thoughts with mindful awareness. You will see the evanescent nature of thoughts, that they are fleeting ideas, all impermanent. And then you can begin to realize that just because you have a thought doesn't mean you have to believe it—much less act on it—and certainly not get caught up in the whole stream of them. You can release the mind of some of its more dangerous patterns. Observing the mind with mindfulness brings liberation.

After you learn to see what's in your mind and learn to release or disidentify with the unhealthy patterns, you discover a deeper level of liberation.

My teacher Sri Nisargadatta explained it like this: "The mind creates the abyss and the heart crosses it." When you rest in the present moment with mindfulness, you open to a presence which is timeless and beyond the understanding of thought. It's by returning to the awareness beyond thoughts that you experience real healing. When your mind and heart open, you realize who you are, the timeless, limitless awareness behind all thought.

Remembering who you really are, you see with the heart. You see the face of someone you love, you see the plum tree that's blooming in front of you. You may be sitting with someone who's grieving or angry, or maybe you're just walking back to your car, but now you're doing it while being fully awake. It's so beautiful to come back to this Earth. Even in great difficulty you can become aware that you are in the presence of mystery, and this experience alone is breathtaking in its power.

For Nisargadatta, the mind creates the abyss of right and wrong, of worries and fears that lead us away from this timeless presence. The only power that can cross this abyss is the awakened heart. Even in difficulty, the awakened heart rests in love.

My teacher Ajahn Chah said it is time to stop the battle with life. "We human beings are constantly in combat, at war, to escape the fact of being limited by circumstances we can't control." Yes we can can tend and love and support all that we care about. But we can't control sickness, old age, and death. We can't control the actions of others. We can't control the actions of our family and loved ones, nor what happens to them. We can't control the actions of our government. We can't control our fate.

Feeling powerless over the most important things in our lives, we struggle, we create suffering. We wage war with others, with events, with anything we don't like. But when we become aware of the often misleading nature of our thoughts, we step outside of the battles they create and see that we are waging a war that we can't win.

To stop the battle and step out of the hypnotism of our thoughts is the liberation of mindfulness of the mind. Mindfulness allows us to know the limits of the thinking mind, to return to the heart. Our heart has spaciousness and love and wisdom and intuition and deep freedom, all of which are beyond all of our stories. "There is in all things an inexhaustible sweetness and purity," writes Thomas Merton, "a silence that is a fountain of action and joy. It rises up in wordless gentleness and flows out to me from the unseen roots of all creation." This is meditation—to rest in the vast silence, which always surrounds us, whether we're aware of it or not.

And in this silence, breath breathes itself, feelings come and go, the body experiences the release of its tensions, and the river of thoughts continues but within a much larger sense of vastness. This is the wisdom that is timeless. It belongs to all living things, and it comes to us naturally, as we practice mindfulness of the mind within the mind.

MINDFULNESS OF THE DHARMA

The last foundation is mindfulness of the dharma in the dharma. *Dharma* is a Sanskrit word that has several meanings. It means truth, it means the path to truth, and it means the elements that make up life. To see the dharma in the dharma means to see the truth of the way things are. In the dharma you see the big picture, the ever-changing play of opposites, the web of birth and death, joy and sorrow, that continuously creates the universe. You see the tentativeness of physical incarnation in this world. You make your peace with the limits of the body. With mindfulness you acknowledge the river of feelings, and the endless play of thoughts. Wakeful and free, you learn to rest in the vastness. This is the dharma in the dharma. You come to realize the essential emptiness of all experience and open to it as it is, ephemeral, ungraspable.

The experience of this letting go opens you to a profound and deep trust in the way things are. Chuang Tzu, the Taoist sage, explained it this way:

A drunken man who falls out of a cart, though he may suffer, does not die. His bones are the same as other people's, but he meets his accident in a different way. His spirit is in a condition of security; he's not conscious of riding in the cart, neither is he conscious of falling out of it. Ideas of life and death, fear, etc., cannot penetrate his breast, and so he does not suffer from contact with objective existence. And if such security is to be got from wine, how much more is it to be got from [the Tao].[5]

Every time you pay attention to this timeless, limitless presence, you become emptier, and the more empty you become, the more healing space there is that can fill with wisdom and love. On the night of his enlightenment, the Buddha saw this truth: that human life by its very nature contains loss and suffering. Human experience is woven out of joy and sorrow, praise and blame, gain and loss, light and dark, hot and cold, pleasure and pain, birth and death. Buddha saw that this is so, that this is the dharma. And as he saw the river of life and its impermanence, he knew that no moment could ever be repeated, and that every moment was always new and that it would quickly end and be replaced by another moment that was also new and would never be repeated, and that it too would be replaced in its turn. And when he saw this and released any desire for life to be different from the way it is, he came to rest in the reality of the present moment. As Zen master Suzuki Roshi explains, "When we realize the 'everlasting truth of everything changes' and find our composure in it, we find ourselves in Nirvana."

There, under the bodhi tree, the Buddha saw the dance of life. He realized he could love it and tend to it, but he couldn't control what was essentially impermanent, and he couldn't fix the fact that it had to contain aging or suffering any more than he could change the reality that life also contains joy and love. The Buddha saw that when the dance of life was lived from a sense of fear, from desires and greed and clinging—that this causes life to be full of hopelessness and struggle, of suffering and confusion.

In the moment of realizing this, he also saw that life was essentially open and free and empty. He understood that freedom is possible for every living being. His sense of fear and grasping fell away. He awakened from the illusion of self, and separation into Nirvana. "You live in illusion and the appearance of things," explains Kalu Rinpoche. "There is a reality, but you do not know this. When you understand this you will see that you are nothing. And being nothing, you are everything. That is all."[6]

This understanding is a direct, immediate experience. You could call it mystical, but it's a natural human experience. We have all tasted moments when our sense of separateness falls away. We experience it sometimes while making love, hiking in the mountains, or listening to great music. There's a part of us that intuits joy and freedom as a possibility and longs to open to it. Sometimes we succeed. But then we forget, or we get lost or confused.

This is like the bear that paced up and down the twenty-foot length of its cage for fifteen years. Finally, the people who ran the zoo realized it was inhumane to keep a wild animal in so small an enclosure. They created a new, larger outdoor space for him. But for the rest of his life the bear continued to pace up and down the same twenty-foot length in the corner as if the cage was still there. We can do the same thing. We can habitually define who we are in a limited way. We live inside our conditioning—our history, our views, our fears—and we forget that this is not who we are. But Buddha's shift of identity from a small sense of self to infinite freedom is possible for all of us. In any moment—even in this one—you can realize your own vastness. With mindfulness of the dharma, you shift from the small sense of self to infinite freedom and presence and timelessness.

And with this openness comes very deep love. You know that you don't possess anything, even your own body, but you know that you have to care for it or you'll create more suffering. You look at your children and realize that you don't own them, and that you cause them and yourself suffering by thinking that you do. Instead, you fully love and care for them and let them live their own lives. And with this simple but profound realization, you become both spacious and more loving.

Chuang Tzu describes this practice:

> If a man is crossing a river and an empty boat collides with his own skiff, they will push it away without shouting or being angry. But if there's a man in the boat, they will shout at him to steer clear and shout, yet again, and become angry and all because there is someone in the boat. Yet, if the boat were empty, they would not be shouting and would not be angry. If you can empty your own boat, crossing the river of the world, no one will oppose you and no one will seek to harm you.[7]

It is important here to clarify what Chuang Tzu means by emptiness, because there are some people who confuse emptiness with deficiency. Deficiency means their boat is full of unworthiness and lack of self-esteem. Chuang Tzu's sense of emptiness is not deficient. It is spacious, open-minded, and resilient. Because it is empty of clinging, it is automatically filled with care.

Chuang Tzu describes a freedom that is mysterious and lovely. Chief Crowfoot gives voice to this: "What is life? It is the flash of a firefly in the night. It is the breath of a buffalo in wintertime. It is the little shadow that runs across the grass and loses itself in the sunset." Life is ephemeral and precious and beautiful and unfathomable. When you open to this mystery, you can awaken mindfulness. You will become liberated from being caught in your fears and confusions and conflicts and attachments.

This doesn't mean that they'll cease to arise. You will continue to experience fears and confusions. Conflict and attachment will continue to show themselves. But you will recognize them for what they are. "Ah, yes, this is fear. I know you. And yes, this is terror. Oh, terror, terror. And this is attachment; this is longing."

You'll get to know them all—the whole menagerie—and you'll also experience the liberation of awareness itself. You'll become intimate with the space of knowing, able to rest in freedom and compassion the same way Buddha did.

When I visited Yeshi Dhonden, during my own medical problems, I could feel him listening with incredible mindfulness to the deep truths of my body. He offered it attention the way my body wanted to be listened to—with openness, wisdom, and compassion. I felt a healing just being in his presence. And in the two years since seeing him I have recovered very well. But in the end you do not need Yeshi Dhonden. You need his attention. Your body wants to be listened to in the same way. With mindfulness you can hold your body with attention and compassion and acceptance. Your feelings want this attention as well, and your mind too.

Everyone around you also wants to be listened to respectfully. This is something that you can offer them no matter what your situation is. This is not some grim duty or an onerous task that you have to do. It's actually very beautiful. It's tough sometimes—because you have to open to things that you might be frightened of—but it's also perfectly safe. For it is this deep attention that brings healing. As a human being, this is what you're supposed to be doing. Your experience of being human in this way—opening to the ten thousand sorrows and joys of yourself and others—becomes a kind of salvation.

A story from the marvelous essayist Lewis Thomas, puts our dance in perspective:

"At home, four p.m. today," says the female moth, and releases a brief explosion of bombykol, a single molecule of which will tremble the hairs of any male within miles and send him driving upwind in a confusion of ardor. But it is doubtful if he has an awareness of being caught in an aerosol chemical attractant. On the contrary, he probably finds, suddenly that it has become an excellent day, the weather remarkably bracing, the time appropriate for a bit of exercise of the old wings, a brisk turn upwind. En route, traveling the gradient of bombykol, he notes the presence of other males, heading in the same direction, all in a good mood, inclined to race for the sheer sport of it. Then, when he reaches his destination, it may seem to him the most extraordinary of coincidences, the greatest piece of luck. "Bless my soul, what have we here?"[8]

These are the same great winds that carry you through life. With mindfulness you can discover that no matter what difficulties you are experiencing, your heart has the capacity to be present, to be compassionate. Wise and free in the winds of life, you can experience the full potential of your humanity. This freedom is your birthright. You know that this is true.

The Return of Joy

*If we cannot be happy in spite of our difficulties,
what good is our spiritual practice?*

Maha Ghosananda, the Gandhi of Cambodia

The practices and teachings in this book invite a beautiful movement of heart, a return to dignity, to the wise and gracious spirit that can be found within you always. When you learn to navigate your difficulties with compassion and grace, you will also discover that joy will return. Yes, life is trouble, as Zorba declares, and yet your difficulties and sorrows do not define you. They do not limit who you are. Sometimes, during periods when your struggles overwhelm you or last for a long time, you can mistake them for your life. You become used to difficulty, you become loyal to your suffering. You don't know who you would be without it. But your difficulties are not the end of the story, they are one part of it—they are part of your path to great love and understanding, a part of the dance of humanity.

When Siddhartha sat by the river at the end of the story by Herman Hesse that many of us read in high school, he finally learned to listen. He realized that all the many voices in the river comprise the music of life: the good and evil, the pleasures and the sorrows, the grief and the laughter, the yearnings and the love. His spirit was no longer in contention with all of life. He found that along with the struggles was also an unshakable joy. This joy can be yours as well.

Maha Ghosananda taught all those he met—including in Cambodia, where almost every family suffered unimaginable losses during the genocide—that in spite of our difficulties, love can return. He taught how to meet sorrows with compassion and understanding, how to honor them, and, finally, how to transform them. It is important not to let your sorrows become your whole life. "When you go to a garden," asks Rumi, "do you look at thorns or flowers? Spend more time with roses and jasmine."

A Buddhist teacher and colleague, Debra Chamberlin-Taylor, tells the story of a community activist who participated in her year-long training group for people of color. This woman had experienced a childhood of poverty, trauma, and abuse. She had faced the death of a parent, illness, divorce from a painful marriage, racism, and the single parenting of two children. She talked about her years of struggle to educate herself, to stand up for what she believed. She described how she had become a radical to fight for justice in local and national politics. Finally, at the last meeting this woman announced, "After all the struggles and troubles I've lived through, I've decided to do something really radical! I am going to be happy."

No matter what you have faced, joy and renewal wait your return. When you remember this, you can open your eyes to the mystery of life around you. Sense the blessings of the Earth in the perfect arc of a ripe tangerine, the taste of warm, fresh bread, the circling flight of birds, the lavender color of the sky shining in a late afternoon rain puddle, the million times we pass other beings, in our cars and shops and out among the trees without crashing, conflict, or harm.

Spiritual practice should not be confused with grim duty. It is the laughter of the Dalai Lama and the wonder born with every child. Maurice Sendak, author of Where the Wild Things Are, depicts this spirit in the story of a boy who wrote to him. "He sent me a charming card with a drawing. I loved it. I answer all my children's letters—sometimes very hastily—but this one I lingered over. I sent him a postcard and I drew a picture of a Wild Thing on it. I wrote, 'Dear Jim, I loved your card.' Then I got a letter back from his mother and she said, 'Jim loved your card so much he ate it.' That to me was one of the highest compliments I've ever received. He didn't care that it was an original drawing or anything. He saw it, he loved it, he ate it."

Yes, we need to carefully navigate through hard times. But the whole world is also our temple, to be tended with love and dignity no matter what. As Martin Luther King Jr. exhorted us all, "If a person sweeps streets for a living, he should sweep them as Michelangelo painted, as Beethoven composed music, as Shakespeare wrote his plays."

The world offers perennial renewal, in the grass that pushes itself up between the cracks in the sidewalk, in the end of every torrential rainstorm and in every newly planted windowbox, in every unexpected revolution, with each new morning's light. This unstoppable spirit of renewal is in you. Trust it. Learn that it flows through you and all of life.

The ultimate gift of our suffering is to teach us how to properly grieve, heal, and learn compassion. But finally we come to the realization that in any moment we can step out of the body of fear and feel the great winds that carry us, to awaken the eternal present. It is within our power to experience the liberation of the heart offered to all by the Buddha in these words:

> *Live in joy,*
> *In love,*
> *Even among those who hate.*
> *Live in joy,*
> *In health,*
> *Even among the afflicted.*
> *Live in joy,*
> *In peace,*
> *Even among the troubled.*
> *Look within.*

Be still.
Free from fear and attachment,
Know the sweet joy of living in the way.

May you be blessed.

Acknowledgments

Enormous gratitude to poet, editor, and steward of the dharma Randy Roark for creating this book out of complicated oral teachings in a lucid and user-friendly form. And bows of deep appreciation to Tami Simon, visionary, friend, and extraordinary upholder of the awakened heart, for her support for me and so many others. A thousand thanks to my sparkling and ever-dedicated assistant, Sara Sparling, cheerful bodhisattva and shepherd of good works. And to my beloved family and colleagues and community members, gratitude for your love and support.

Notes

Chapter 1: The Wisdom of Our Difficulties

1. Elie Wiesel, *A Jew Today* (New York: Random House Digital, Inc., 1979).

Chapter 2: The Earth Is My Witness

1. Tamara Engle, New York Insight Meditation Center, personal communication.

2. Shunryu Suzuki, ed. Trudy Dixon, *Zen Mind, Beginner's Mind* (Boston: Shambhala Publications, 2010), 24.

Chapter 3: Shared Compassion

1. D. S. Barnett, "Readers Write: Fears and Phobias," *The Sun* 314 (2002): 30.

Chapter 7: The Zen of an Aching Heart

1. Graf Durckheim, *The Way of Transformation: Daily Life as Spiritual Exercise* (London: Allen & Unwin, 1988), 81–82.

Chapter 8: Equanimity and Peace

1. Adapted from Stephen Mitchell, *Tao Te Ching* (New York: HarperPerennial, 1992).

Chapter 9: Your Highest Intention

1. Thomas Merton, ed. William H. Shannon, *The Hidden Ground of Love: The Letters of Thomas Merton on Religious Experience and Social Concerns* (New York: Macmillan, 1986), 294.

Chapter 10: The Four Foundations of Mindfulness and the Healing Journey

1. Richard Selzer, *Mortal Lessons: Notes on the Art of Surgery* (New York: Houghton Mifflin Harcourt, 1996), 33–36.

2. Lauren Slater, *Welcome to My Country: A Therapist's Memoir of Madness* (New York: Anchor books/Doubleday 1997), xiii.

3. Jack Kornfield, *After the Ecstasy, the Laundry: How the Heart Grows Wise on the Spiritual Path* (New York: Bantam Books, 2000), 180.

4. Jack Kornfield, *A Path with Heart: A Guide Through the Perils and Promises of Spiritual Life* (New York: Bantam Books, 1993), 116.

5. Chuang Tzu, Zhuangzi, *Teachings and Sayings of Chuang Tzu* (Toronto: Dover Editions, 2001), 31.

6. Jack Kornfield, *The Buddha Is Still Teaching: Contemporary Buddhist Wisdom* (Boston: Shambhala Publications, 2010), 3.

7. Thomas Merton, *The Way of Chuang Tzu* (Boston: Shambhala Publications, 2004), 131.

8. Lewis Thomas, *The Lives of a Cell, Notes of a Biology Watcher* (New York: Bantam Books, 1975), 18.

About the Author

Jack Kornfield, PhD, trained as a Buddhist monk in Thailand, Burma, and India. He is cofounder of the Insight Meditation Society in Massachusetts and the Spirit Rock Meditation Center in California and is one of the key teachers to introduce mindfulness meditation to the West. His books include *The Wise Heart: A Guide to the Universal Teachings of Buddhist Psychology; Teachings of the Buddha; A Path with Heart; After the Ecstasy, the Laundry; and Living Dharma*. His books have been translated into twenty languages and have sold more than a million copies. A father and husband, Jack holds a PhD in clinical psychology, and he teaches and lives in Woodacre, California.

About Sounds True

Sounds True is a multimedia publisher whose mission is to inspire and support personal transformation and spiritual awakening. Founded in 1985 and located in Boulder, Colorado, we work with many of the leading spiritual teachers, thinkers, healers, and visionary artists of our time. We strive with every title to preserve the essential "living wisdom" of the author or artist. It is our goal to create products that not only provide information to a reader or listener, but that also embody the quality of a wisdom transmission.

For those seeking genuine transformation, Sounds True is your trusted partner. At SoundsTrue.com you will find a wealth of free resources to support your journey, including exclusive weekly audio interviews, free downloads, interactive learning tools, and other special savings on all our titles.

To learn more, please visit SoundsTrue.com or call us toll free at 800.333.9185.

Guided versions of the meditations "Zen and the Aching Heart" and "Your Highest Intention" are available at SoundsTrue.com/bonus/Jack _Kornfield_dark.

SOUNDS TRUE
many voices, one journey